Broken to Whole:

Inner Healing for the Fragmented Soul

Written by:

Seneca Schurbon, Diane Moyer,

Michael C. King, Matt Evans,

Sam R. Brewster & Ruby Hunter

Available from Amazon.com, Createspace.com, and other retail outlets where applicable.

ISBN-13: 978-1-912045-66-2
ISBN-10: 1912045664

Table of Contents

Disclaimers

Medical Disclaimer

None of the authors of this book are licensed psychological clinicians, and none of the stories, opinions, or ideas shared here are specifically endorsed by any governing medical body of any kind. The ideas shared here are anecdotal and are meant to serve as an adjunct or unlicensed complement to any professional therapy the reader may undertake. Additionally, this book is not a substitute for treatment under a licensed clinician nor does purchasing or reading this material constitute as creating a client-practitioner relationship. While some of the authors do offer products and services, these are not a substitute for medical treatment.

Theological Disclaimer

One of the challenges this book presented to us, the writers, is that we all come from different backgrounds with different perspectives. Some of us came from more liturgical backgrounds with Catholic and Episcopal upbringings while others grew up in other Christian denominations, agnosticism, or otherwise broad and undefined spirituality. What this means is that the views shared here are extremely varied.

The coauthors do not necessarily agree with all the views held by the other coauthors as written in these pages. We value and respect one another and trust that each is doing his or her best to follow where the Lord leads, no matter how odd and challenging others may think their journey. God has led each of us in new directions and in various ways over the years, and we are all still in search of greater understanding of so many things related to these topics. We each walk in arenas today that we did not have a grid for ten to fifteen years ago, and this book is a perfect example of that. In some cases, we still feel we are creating the roadmap as we go. What this means for you is that even if we don't all see eye-to-eye on everything, we are giving one another grace to pursue Jesus in the unique way He is leading them. We invite you to do the same.

We have compiled this book with the name of the coauthor in the subheading, allowing the reader to navigate the various voices as you read. Incidentally, if you feel that you more closely identify with an author and his or her perspective, you can easily find that content in the book. If you struggle with some information, you can just leave that part and look for what you need elsewhere so that you can receive healing.

We fully trust God will meet you where you are.

Our Terminology vs. Medical Terminology

The American Psychological Association and related clinicians typically refer to some of the subjects we discuss in this book as dissociation. Common medical terms for this type of condition are Dissociative Identity Disorder (DID) and the older term, Multiple Personality Disorder (MPD), where a single person has had, through traumatic events or chemical means, their brain and/or soul fracture into multiple parts, each with some semblance of sentience and personality. Most commonly, the average person will not have experienced anything similar to these diagnoses, but we maintain that soul trauma exists on a spectrum and that all of us can benefit from healing and integration work even if we have not been medically diagnosed with DID.

Even medical professionals disagree on the exact meanings of some psychological conditions, so we have simplified the terminology and definitions for any of the potential psychological conditions or situations one may experience. These include apparent alternate personalities, fractured consciousness, repressed memories, or similar diagnoses, and we will consistently refer to them all with three interchangeable terms: fragments, parts, or storage cubbies.

Some professionals use other terms, such as alters, meaning "alternate personalities," which describe similar conditions or psychological circumstances, but for simplicity's sake, we will aim to stick with the terms mentioned above unless otherwise specified. For our purposes in this book, we do not find any advantages to drawing lines and attempting to determine the defining line between a fragment and an alter nor are we clinically qualified to do so. Please note that our terms do not imply any standard or diagnosis. While all alters are "parts," not all parts are "alters."

Impartation to the Reader

As we were nearing the end of this book, I (Seneca) came across a prophetic word that seems perfectly fitting for what you're about to read. It was describing a game of hot potato played among many participants, none of whom wanted to hold onto a "hot topic." As they flung it from person to person, each one only held it for a moment and certainly did not receive any nourishment. I grabbed a pair of oven mitts and stepped in. "I'll take it! I can handle it!"

Since I initiated this project and invited these authors to join me, life has heated up. In your hands—or on your e-reader, as the case may be—you hold a hot potato of revelation. As such, I bequeath to you, dear reader, spiritual oven mitts. Others have instantly dropped some of the topics in this book, forfeiting any benefit. I invite you to put on your protection and hold some of these concepts long enough to really see them, to judge rather than react, let them sink in a bit, and then dig in. Apply these truths as you minister first to yourself and then, to others. Do some intentional damage to the kingdom of darkness and bring freedom to the captives!

Introduction

We, the authors, would like to welcome you to what could be possibly the strangest non-fiction book you have ever read. This book will most likely challenge your beliefs and stretch your understanding of the inner world of emotional trauma, but we trust it will also inform you and draw you further down the path to wholeness. If you are new to inner healing, deliverance (also known as exorcism or casting out demons), or the spiritual realm as a whole, this book will seem fantastical in parts, but we assure you that it is not a joke nor are we making up anything.

Our central premise is that through the journey of our lives, especially during our formative years, we experience wounds, known in some circles as fractured parts, fragments, soul splinters, split parts, etc.

When we undergo a traumatic event, our minds and/or souls break off little parts of themselves as a protective mechanism, hiding away the memories and pain of the incident to help us cope with the trauma so that we can function normally in life. The solution to this problem is to identify these fragmented pieces of the soul, heal them, and then reattach or integrate them into the core self.

Fragments can manifest as overreactions or childish behavior in certain circumstances even as an adult. Sabotaged relationships, missing memories, impulsivity, or inexplicable strong reactions to specific places are possible indicators of fragments. Whether you have experienced this to date or not, we believe everyone has at least one of these parts that can be integrated back into the whole and will be able to benefit from the information shared in this book.

If you have been through the gamut of inner healing methods, ministries, and techniques, yet still have unresolved pain, this is a must read. The "missing pieces" you've been looking for so that you can complete your healing might literally be just that—missing pieces.

This is not about saying magic words and believing until you're healed. "Fake it 'til you make it" hasn't worked for any of us, and we don't expect it to work for you, either. You might have even been through ministry that has addressed fragments. They likely prayed a prayer with you at some point in your session and told you to believe by faith that the pieces were all integrated. They might have patted you on the back and told you that you should be all better. Our guess is that if you've picked up this book, you're still hurting. If you have repented your "repenter" off, stood on all the right Scriptures, prayed all the right prayers, waited in every ministry line, and you're still here, still carrying the pain, you are the reason we wrote this book.

The only magic bullet we know of is Jesus, and we have collaborated on some different exercises and techniques with loads of real life examples to empower you, the reader, to receive the emotional healing you want and need. As you begin to put these truths into practice in your own life, you'll be able to help others as well.

Section 1:

Trauma 101

Chapter 1: Sam

Trauma and How Parts are Formed

All of us experience trauma. In our conscious minds, we tend to grade traumatic events according to severity, especially looking back at our childhoods. We also tend to compare our traumas with those of others. In some sense, trauma is quantifiable. Rape or murder is more significant than breaking a bone while skiing, which is again more serious than someone making fun of your hair. The difficulty with this comparison or quantification is that it tends to reduce the importance of the "lesser" events to insignificance. As a result, people become stuck and ignore their issues because, "At least it wasn't as bad as X, Y, or Z." If something continues to influence your decisions or behavior, then it is significant, and healing will work to powerfully allow you greater freedom to be who you were created to be without inner hurts guiding your life choices.

For the sake of this discussion, I'm going to use the term 'trauma' to refer to anything that was negative or upsetting when it happened. We'll address the greater scope of the continuum in a little bit.

Trauma happens. How it affects you will depend on many different factors unique to you, including your personality, the time, and the situation. Trauma produces negative emotions relating to the event, the people involved, and ourselves. We store those emotions in our bodies. The trauma can color how we view others or ourselves. All of those aspects can be entry points for the enemy's lies and attachments. He is evil, and he is always ready and waiting to kick us when we're down.

We might believe lies about people, places, situations, and our identity and purpose. We sometimes come into agreement with the enemy and make vows about situations or people. We make these agreements in an attempt to protect ourselves from further pain.

When emotions overwhelm us, we might split off a part of our soul to hold them. I like to call them 'storage cubbies' because they function as a little locker in your soul that stores all of that pain, anger, sadness, or any other emotion we either can't handle or have determined not to feel. These seem to be extremely common if not normative.

I've heard from several sources that a person does not form fragments after childhood; while I understand why experts believe that, I'm not entirely sure that this is true. Fragments do seem to form more frequently when you are young, and perhaps the ability or propensity to split begins early or not at all. I'm not sure that the exact timing matters a great deal. If you tend to have extreme and abnormally strong reactions to certain events, then the event might possibly trigger an unhealed wound from the past. When you react to the event today, you are actually tapping into the pain from the previous event and in some ways, reliving it, which is what causes your response.

What has happened in this instance is that your subconscious filed that event in your mind under "trauma." You didn't know how to cope with the overwhelming emotions that came from this traumatic event, so you created a little storage compartment in your soul to hold or contain them. This is the most common form of dissociation, and nearly everyone does this to some extent. You stuff emotions into an internal compartment, and you shut the door.

The problem is that the door doesn't lock. You might think that it has, but it hasn't. As other, similar traumas happen, you store more emotions in that same locker. They might stay hidden, but they cannot heal in the locker.

I am an occupational therapist by training, and while I do not currently practice as one, I worked for many years in hospitals. One of the areas I trained in was wound care. If you receive a deep wound, your body's natural response is to cover the wound as quickly as possible, growing new skin cells to cover it. The problem for deep wounds, though, is that those skin cells can trap dead tissue and bacteria within the wound, allowing an infection to grow.

This is often how I picture what these storage cubbies do. They cover the wound so that you can move forward as if all is well. As with deep wounds that create new skin, they look fine on the surface, but they do not allow the wound to heal. Thus, when you experience something hurtful, your reaction is out of proportion to the current event because you are not just reacting to it in the moment, but you are tapping into all of the woundedness that lies underneath it from past events.

For some reason, although this is less common, you can also have a generational component to these storage cubbies or other fragments. How this happens is less clear. Sometimes, clients appear to have woundedness that has been passed down, so not only do they react to the wounding of the moment, but to all of the hurts of their ancestors as well. You will often find familial spirits of one sort or another involved here, so I'm not sure if the actual storage cubby itself is passed down or if the entity creates one as part of its activities in the person's life. I wish that I understood more about this field with greater clarity. It's the scientist in me, I suppose, but I would love to know the how and the why of it all.

As much as I like to understand these things, often understanding how it happens doesn't matter. Sometimes the why is important, but even then, general knowledge about the issue is typically sufficient. What to do with a storage cubby once you suspect that it is there remains fairly consistent, regardless of individual details. While my curiosity is left unsatisfied, people are still able to find freedom, which is the most important thing.

These fractured parts can have increasing levels of sentience and ability to interact with the authentic self. On the more significant end, some can actually take over the person's body with or without the authentic self being aware of what has happened. There seems to be some correlation between the severity of the trauma and the degree of autonomy the part might have.

All parts have this in common—they have all yielded ownership of part of the soul, generally to the enemy. They are created to assist the authentic self in surviving trauma—at least, that's the intention at the time. It sounds like a good idea, and it does work, at least partially.

The problem with the higher functioning parts seems fairly obvious. When they take over, your authentic self is not always the one in control of what you are doing, saying, etc. This can cause issues with relationships and in the workplace when one of your parts surfaces that acts and performs vastly differently than the authentic self. However, even when storage cubbies are on the "milder" side, the problem is that part of the soul is held hostage by those emotions. As long as the emotions are not dealt with, that part of your soul is stuck at whatever age you were when it was formed.

In the case of fragments, and especially storage cubbies, the healing process is usually nowhere near as traumatic or as lengthy as physical healing from big injuries. The process is fairly straight forward, and we'll talk about that more as the book progresses.

Chapter 2: Diane

Introduction to Fragments

I've often taken people in prayer back to the womb to pre-birth memories for the sake of healing the root of their issues. When I came to the relevant area in the womb where a person needed ministry, I asked the Lord to heal that problem. Then, I wouldn't look for any further matters in utero after they received healing in that one area. I ended the prayer session right there.

Years ago, through a personal healing experience, the Lord showed me that this was incomplete as it left the person without full healing.

During a time of personal crisis in which I knew I was operating out of woundedness, I called a prayer counselor friend and asked her to pray with me. She felt that I needed to go back to the womb for ministry. I had gone to the womb for healing previously, but I did it again because I trusted her discernment. I discovered some issues that had happened in utero about the third month, and we continued to process through additional issues until birth. Afterward, I watched in the spirit as that part or aspect of me grew up and was integrated into the rest of me. I felt it. I was surprised because I had no idea that this part existed.

I felt that there was more to this experience. I started praying and seeking the Lord about it, and he showed me the Scriptures about double-mindedness in James 1:8 that says, "being a double-minded man, unstable in all his ways." I looked up 'double-minded,' and the root of 'minded' is 'psyche,' which means soul. 'Double' means twice, so being double minded means you have two souls. Hmmm . . . how can that be? Two souls?

The Lord showed me that what I had been taught before about double-mindedness—one foot in him, one foot in the world—was not correct. 'Double-mindedness' means two souls or two minds. What I felt the Lord was revealing to me was that many people have a part or parts of their soul that were stuck in trauma while they were a child. This fractured-off part of ourselves speaks within us—an internal voice that wants its own way.

A training I took years ago taught that when something painful happens to us as a child, a part of our soul may become emotionally stuck at that stage of development, which might be why an adult becomes angry and starts to act like a young child. Another example is with child molesters. They tend to target the age when they were abused and wounded themselves. If you are working with a molester who has abused a four-year-old, then you need to look into what happened to him when he was the same age.

When we are hurt/wounded, a fragment of our identity becomes stuck at that point in the memory. The fragment is a part of the authentic, original person we were at that age with the same belief system we had at that age as well. This part might not believe in God at all, or it might be resentful of him because of what happened. This part still influences and speaks to us within. We often think it's the Devil, ignore it, or give in to it. Many of these parts are located on

24

the right side of our brain. The right side of our brain cannot process time, so any part found there will be outside of time, stuck in the same period when the event occurred.

More recently, the Lord gave me a picture of what fragments/fractured parts are. He has been showing me that although our body is one, it has many parts—fingers, toes, arms, head, eyes, etc. Each part has its function and job (1 Corinthians 12:14-26). Our soul functions in a similar manner—it is one but has many parts, each with its own function. If you break an arm, you find ways to compensate, doing what you normally would do without using that arm. If you lose your eyesight, then your other senses become more enhanced to help you function. Although this works to some degree, it is never the same or as effective as if you were not injured.

The soul works the same way. When we are wounded emotionally, a part of our soul is crippled. We developed defense and coping mechanisms to overcome the crippling in that part of the soul. These mechanisms remain in place until that part of the soul is healed.

You cannot talk or decide your way out of this kind of problem, and self-control only works for a short while. The Lord ministering to the wounded part of the soul is the best solution.

Remember that your fragments have the same identity and belief system as you did when the event occurred. If you were two at the time, then the fragments believe what you did at two. They are there to protect you. You are important to them although some might harbor some resentment that you went on with your life while they are still stuck in the past memory.

Fragments and alters are not our enemies. They are not to be feared, hated, or resented. They are parts of ourselves that have been trapped in a traumatic/abusive memory for years. They cannot escape the memory—it is constant for them. They have not moved forward, and the pain is as fresh for them today as when the event happened.

You will find that many fragments are incredibly tired. It is tiring to be in constant pain. When they are out, you will feel tired, which is a sign that they are present. Love your fragments and alters—they have done you a great service. They have carried a burden that you could not and have helped you for years. In this regard, they are a lot like Jesus, carrying your pain and sorrows as He carries them. Thank them for a job well done, then introduce them to Jesus because He is so thankful for them. He wants to see them healed and delivered even more than they do. He loves them so much and is happy they are there. After all, He created us with the ability to develop these parts so that we could continue to live on after something horrible happens to us. He appreciates them and wants them to feel better.

Chapter 3: Matt

Heading off the Beaten Path

I began moving in physical healing and simple deliverance at a young age in response to some spiritual experiences where I became convinced that the Lord was "calling" me to operate in those ministries. Before that, I had no idea that such things were possible for me, and I had no intentions of pursuing them. I lacked the foundational understanding of the Gospel that I have today that tells me that "as he is, so also are we in this world" (1 John 4:17), that we are all meant to operate in everything Jesus did and even more (John 14:12, etc.).

As I stepped out regularly in physical healing and deliverance, I learned how awesome our authority in Christ is and how our faith can consistently move the Spirit of God to change physical realities before our very eyes. There is nothing like watching physical bodies transform from broken to whole, from paralyzed to functioning, from blind to seeing, or from bruised and battered to fresh—all of this occurring right in front of you as if no harm had ever happened to them, confirming the reality of God's promises to every believer.

There is also nothing like seeing demonic entities manifest up close and personal, watching them bow the knee to the Name of Jesus, setting a person free to make the reality of the spiritual realm come alive. It is one thing to "know your identity and authority in Christ" as merely a doctrine in your head, but it is another thing altogether to experience this confirmed in physical reality and in the lives of people today.

I discovered that one couldn't progress very far with praying for physical healing before being met by the demonic working to resist healing. In some cases, people needed deliverance to obtain their healing. I found that I had much to learn in that realm, only to discover that one could only progress so far in deliverance without resolving underlying emotional issues. I had even more to learn about that subject.

Today, I give minimal attention to the demonic, except as necessary, and primarily focus on healing the person's deeper issues. This seems to be the biggest area where folks need help, and as a person's issues are resolved, the demonic loses all ability to resist a quick, single command of authority in Christ to go.

I've found the healing of fractured parts to be a necessity for most people when it comes to resolving many deeper emotional issues. I even pray with those who have gone through much conventional inner healing spanning years or decades who have never received healing for their most significant hurts until they began healing their fractured parts. This is just one of the many facets of deeper healing and transformation paid for us through the work of the cross.

Learning What Not to Do

I attended Spirit-filled churches for a number of years. I experienced a lot of positives, but I was also exposed to many traditional mentalities about how people are expected to become healed or set free from what troubled them. I discovered that many "revival" and "gospel" ministries that are meant to free people actually placed unrealistic burdens on them.

Some ministries seemed to expect that a quick time of repentance and a brief prayer at an altar was enough to fix people. They tended to quote Scripture verses, such as, "The yoke shall be broken because of the anointing," and "Behold, I do a new thing! Remember not the former things, says the Lord," from Isaiah. All you needed, they thought, was someone to lay hands on you, speak the name of Jesus, impart the power of Holy Spirit, and you would then be free from everything that bothered you—if you were genuinely repentant.

We experienced a real touch from God in those places, such as maybe falling down and getting the shakes or having a supernatural sense of His joy and His closeness to us. This is not to be underestimated, but it usually didn't equal healing of our issues or of anything approaching full spiritual freedom. God likes to be with us, to share His joy of having relationship with us, to make us feel good, and He doesn't always need to fix us at the time. Just like any quality relationship you have with any other person, you won't always spend your time fixing each other.

However, many religious folks expected us to be fixed after such an experience. The truth was that we still had most of the same issues we had come in with, but now we "had no excuse!" I can't count how many people I've known who have been given worthless and ineffective answers to their hurts and then were condemned for not being totally healed.

In my case, I was dealing with deep woundedness in some seriously fractured parts of myself. To find real healing, I wasn't going to be able to decide one day to "repent" or to "just get over it." A little touch from the Lord on the surface wasn't enough. I was going

29

to need to open up long blocked-off areas of my heart and allow Him to work progressively in those places.

I came to find far greater breakthrough for both myself and others by learning to apply more in-depth knowledge and wisdom in partnership with Holy Spirit. He has called us to a participatory role. He has called us to learn how to exercise the authority and inheritance He has given us in Christ. It has definitely been a process with lots of trial and error along the way but with continual and awesome progress. I love seeing actual transformation in people's lives rather than just a showy spiritual touch on the surface, especially when folks are desperate for real change.

In later years, I ran across ministries who thought you only needed to know a certain doctrine—your identity in Christ, the grace message and the work of the cross, the Father heart of God, or some such thing, and that this "new revelation" would solve all your problems. People did learn positive thinking and some healthy self-esteem, sometimes even experiencing real spiritual breakthroughs due to the teaching of core Gospel truths, but many folks' deeper issues stayed the same as they had always been.

At first, such oversimplified belief systems—that you only needed a new doctrine or way of thinking—tempted us with a shortcut to freedom yet actually caused many to stagnate long term. Folks were attempting to deny the reality of their woundedness rather than opening up to the Lord so that He could truly heal it. This produced cultures of hypocrisy where many people obviously acted out of deeper issues, hurting one another grievously, and destroying relationships in the same ways over and over again, yet their belief systems didn't allow them to admit that they had any remaining brokenness.

The more severely hurting people found out very quickly that believing doctrines didn't heal their deeper woundedness. They felt like the Gospel apparently worked for everyone except them because others could pretend to have it all together for a while longer than they could.

Confident reassertions were made to the deeply wounded that they only needed to change their thinking, and all would be well. Try as they might, these people discovered that no amount of work on their thinking resolved their torment. They were blamed for "not having enough faith" or for "finding their identity from their issues rather than in Christ," yet their faith level or sense of identity was usually not the true culprits. Instead, people needed actual healing, not just pat answers and condemnation.

Just knowing a doctrine about our identity or about the goodness of God isn't the same as actually experiencing those realities through a heart-transforming encounter. When we experience real healing, we will know the heart of God and our identity in Christ from the deepest core of our being rather than only knowing these things intellectually. The Lord would rather that we know and walk with Him from a healed and whole heart than to merely force our broken hearts to comply against their will to dry doctrines in our heads.

"Salvation" in scripture is translated from the Greek word "sozo," which means healing and deliverance. It is often used in places where it couldn't possibly mean anything but immediate physical healing or immediate deliverance from oppression. The salvation Jesus died to give us was not meant to be only received as a hope for the afterlife or a head trip about having it all together but is meant to be actual healing and transformation here and now.

Ministry to fractured parts was a basic element of Jesus' mission statement in Luke 4:18. There, he quoted Isaiah 61, "The Spirit of the Lord God is upon me, because he has anointed me to preach good news to the poor, he has sent me to bind up/heal the broken hearted..." The word for "broken hearted" there in the Hebrew is "shabar," which means to be shattered into many pieces. Jesus came to heal and to bind together those who have been shattered into many pieces. We've found this to be literally true; most, if not all, people have been shattered into many fractured parts, and these parts need to be healed and joined back together for the person to experience wholeness. Healing for fractured parts not only became a very important part of my own journey but has become a key aspect of my ministry to others today, and I run into more people who need help than I can personally minister to.

Experiencing It for Myself

I began learning about this subject while searching out answers for folks who were dealing with more difficult issues than mine. I was led to answers in the form of basic ministry to fractured parts, finding along the way that I needed ministry in that area myself. Some of my own nearly instantaneous experiences of healing in this area were so dramatic that I felt I could barely relate to various ways I had perceived myself and the world around me only seconds prior. My emotions and perspectives changed significantly and instantly during larger integrations, and this happened not just once but multiple times.

In one early healing session, two men from a ministry team called up a certain fractured part. Immediately, I was in another state of mind, experiencing that part's consciousness. I was seeing into the spiritual realm as clearly as we normally see into the natural realm, and I had a sensation of rapidly spinning around.

Above my head—my part's head—was this contraption with flashing lights all over it that looked like something out of Star Trek. It seemed to be responsible for the spinning. As soon as I shared this, one of the team members prayed for the sci-fi-looking device to be destroyed. Immediately, the rapid spinning sensation stopped as the overhead contraption disappeared. Their opinion was that this device related to programming that goes on during ritual abuse (RA) although I have never been ritually abused.

They questioned this part of me and led it in prayer for healing and integration, quickly walking it through a few steps of healing and then integrating it. The feeling of integration is hard to describe because I cannot compare it to anything else. However, I would say that I seemed to be significantly more self-aware after the experience as if there was 'more' of me. I felt as if I had new capacities. For the rest of that day, I also felt as if I was being spun in the opposite direction from how my part was previously spinning during the session. This was probably because this part was so used to being spun one way that being still now felt like spinning the other way. A major sense of oppression lifted from me during that ministry time as well.

The explanation I was given for the RA-related contraption was that some programming is put upon people without a need for physical contact when rituals are done through astral projection. When I searched through materials on ritual abuse years later, I also found out that spinning is a known RA technique to create dissociation.

While this is interesting information, I don't think I can draw hard conclusions about exactly how I got all those fractured parts or why my healing process was more complicated than I would have expected. Most of my healing sessions were more subtle than the one I just described, yet the results were sometimes very significant. Emotional issues instantly resolved. The way I felt around people and related to them suddenly changed, becoming healthier. I found rest in areas where I was previously stressed out and driven.

In another session, many of my parts were being brought out from all kinds of different hiding places: underground, underwater, caves, dungeons, etc. One was even trapped in a dungeon with a territorial spirit connected to it by a giant insect-type stinger stuck into

, back. This was dismantled easily through a quick prayer, and the part was brought out of the dungeon just as quickly.

To work with the large crowd of parts, the minister used an older, more whole and stronger part as a liaison, who he called up via a word of knowledge by the name "Steven." I just followed his leading, allowing the thoughts and impressions within me to come to the surface, sharing them with this minister. Pretty soon, the session was off and running. Interestingly, when I was very young, about five or six, I tended to make up stories about a person named "Steven/Stephen." Although I pronounced his name "Steven," I spelled it "Stephen." This person had all sorts of adventures in my young imagination as a very capable and heroic type of character.

This fractured part of me who responded to that name felt very mature and turned out to be a great communicator for the rest of my parts. He flowed exceptionally well in discernment and prophecy and understood ministry to parts very well. This was a few years into my journey, and I already had some experience working with parts. I was a young adult at the time, so I wondered if this might have been my "ministry fragment" that I switched to when I wanted to let go of awareness of everything else in my life so that I could just flow in the Spirit. He seemed to be me at my best in that area, and it was so easy for him.

Steven was rattling off discernment after discernment of what was going on with the rest of my parts, identifying issue after issue among the younger parts and what the Lord wanted to do for them, then what needed to be done next, etc. The minister leading the session had little to do as this part quickly pointed out how the Lord was saying this and healing that and so on, just as if he'd done this all a thousand times before.

More parts—single, in pairs, or in entire groups—were called together from various places, brought out of hiding places, or rescued from captivity to join the larger crowd. Steven identified the types and colors of clothes they were wearing and what problems those colors represented. He explained how the Lord was ministering to those parts to change all the clothes to white, representing spiritual purity, and/or simply describing the various issues they were being healed from and how that was being done. The large group of parts, including Steven, were all healed from various issues and integrated during that short session that lasted roughly one hour. It made a significant difference for me.

At times, I prayed for my own parts without help, perceiving them in the spirit and asking the Lord to walk them through healing and integration. I often noticed a shift taking place inside me, and in the case of larger parts or groups of parts, I experienced a sense of confusion for a few hours afterward as integration was being processed. After more significant integrations, I also noticed even more of a sense of confusion before positive changes later manifested in my life.

Those are a few examples of what healing and integration for fractured parts looked like for me. Overall, this was tremendously valuable in bringing healing to me in many areas. Most of these were areas where I had no idea that I needed help. I only discovered that I was different or healthier after they were healed. Some of what I was healed from were even areas that I thought were positive qualities until I discovered that they suddenly changed (for the better) after integration. In other words, this was not healing that came from analysis of memories or of personal problems, from sorting out lies from truth on the level of the intellect, but healing that happened miraculously and on a very deep level, regardless of my own cognitive understanding at the time. These were not issues related to my conscious thinking but were deeper aspects of me that needed to be healed over which I had no conscious control.

One unexpected result of all this healing was the fading away of the driven intensity and performance-orientation typical of my previous persona. I became much more laid back and no longer felt such a deep need to "have it all together" in order to be okay with myself. I became content to be someone in the middle of a process. I was now able to just receive grace and love on a deep level despite the fact that I still had many issues and even sins. I no longer felt the need to always be accomplishing something "great" in order to be happy with who I was.

I wasn't perfectly healed from perfectionism after this, but I was suddenly a lot farther down the road than I had been, and the change was at a much deeper level than my thinking.

Dissociation might look like shutting off a broken part of ourselves, shoving it beneath our consciousness, or becoming driven to think and to prove that we have it all together. We might try to actualize some achievement, showing that we aren't the horrible person a suppressed part of us feels that we are. A difficulty with this might be that the people who are most heavily dissociated are also the most driven to never admit to themselves that they have any real issues, especially (gasp!) fractured parts.

Healing in this area will likely remove a decent amount of our motivation to live up to an idealized standard. We start to become okay with being weak in many places and with facing the fact that we are failing in many ways, knowing that Daddy still loves us and is with us. This frees us much more to receive grace where we are at and to walk out the destiny the Lord has for us, even if it might not be something flashy or high profile, according to popular opinion. When we receive healing in this area, we will then no longer seek to prove things to others or even to ourselves as much.

While walking out this healing, I even felt like a child for a time and related to people in a very childlike way. This was not well received by some of the legalistic, performance-driven types around me. They seemed to think that I was backsliding because I was no longer running on the same hamster wheels they were on. Some of them pressured me to climb back under their guilt-driven performance trips again, but I don't think I could have done that if I had tried. All I could do was enjoy the fact that God loved me—just like a simple child— regardless of what my performance looked like to others or to myself. I believe that was a processing phase because I balanced out somewhere in-between those two extreme states of driven perfectionism vs. simple childishness as time went by. I still had tons of progress to make in many other areas, but, in and of itself, this was a major breakthrough.

Healing looks different for different people, and I have yet to find someone whose process has looked exactly like mine. I have found that all kinds of emotional issues can be resolved through healing fractured parts: severe depression, overwhelming fear and anxiety, out-of-control anger, shame and low self-esteem, and the general feeling of powerlessness and helplessness in daily situations. These and many more have been turned around, sometimes completely, through just this one area of ministry.

As I continued praying with folks and working with their fractured parts, I found that many, many people seemed to benefit.

Chapter 4: Seneca

I'm Not As Weird As I Think

My introduction to fractured parts was gradual. Looking back, I see that I had an undercurrent of awareness. I make flower essences, which are different than essential oils, for emotional healing. One of my jobs is writing what each flower does, and as I did so for particular flowers, I later realized that I was describing the healing of fractured parts before I even understood what that was.

Later on, I was trained in a couple of different inner-healing modalities, each having their own way of dealing with parts, but I didn't really grab a hold of either method.

Parts also became evident in dreams, and when I started accidentally interacting with them in the spirit realm, that's when I buckled down and knew that this was a form of healing I needed to pursue. The experiences I was having were completely off my grid until I met these crazy people I'm writing this book with.

For the most part, I was keeping my weird spiritual experiences to myself. God occasionally dropped unexpected spiritual encounters on me, and I ended up ministering to people in the spirit. That is still the only way I minister to others outside of what I do with essences—with no involvement from the other party. This set me up perfectly for what would follow.

I went public on social media with an issue I was having. Every time God prompts me to tell my story, I never understand why, but it always ends up having a huge impact. An acquaintance contacted me as a result and confessed to being a bit invasive and going into the spirit realm to see what I was dealing with and to find out how he could help. He described what he saw, what he did, and what happened, and had I not already had some similar experiences with other people in the spirit realm, I might not have been as receptive to what he described.

Shortly after, co-authors Matt and Diane ministered to me tag-team style regarding the issue. Afterward, I faced an adjustment period where I struggled with how to "be." I was a bit disconcerted to feel so little and not be in the process of an emotional bleed-out all day everyday while this trigger was in my face. I could have been happy, but I was genuinely concerned. (I've grown pretty comfortable since.) Issues did flare up a bit here and there after that session, but I spoke on the phone with one or the other of them and kept working through it.

In a way, the language of fractured parts makes sense. It's engrained in our everyday language. "A part of me still feels _____." It's the inner conflicts; it's when strong emotions run the show. It's when a suppressed side of one's self breaks free and has an outburst because it cannot be contained any longer. It's why we sabotage relationships, play it safe, or make detrimental decisions. We cannot find internal unity as long as we have split parts.

When trauma happens, and parts are created, one of their jobs is to keep you safe, so they hang out under the surface until a situation that resembles the original trauma presents itself.

40

When you are in a new situation that your fragment associates with the initial trauma, even if it is a scaled-down version, that part will make sure that you realize how unsafe the situation is. You'll re-live all the original emotions connected to the initial trauma as if the past is present. The reason this happens is so that you'll go into "fight or flight" mode and come out in one piece, unlike last time.

This protective mechanism works until you are in perfectly safe circumstances, yet because of your history, you go into a fight or flight mode anyway. Depending on what you've been through in the past, this might make it difficult to maintain healthy relationships, keep a job if it triggers you on an ongoing basis, or deal with any other areas of life that mimic old trauma.

Chapter 5: Michael Signs You Might Have Fragments

This chapter title is a bit misleading because, in the opinion of this author, every human alive has various parts that need integration. With that said, definite indicators exist that point to fragments playing a more active part in a person's life. Sometimes these can go unnoticed on a day-to-day basis, but at other times, they completely disrupt normal life. Regardless of where one falls on the spectrum, fragments need to be healed and integrated, but diagnosis is a key first step. When I say diagnosis here, I am not referring to that of a licensed clinician but rather basic recognition of a problem because, as the saying goes, we can't solve a problem that we don't know exists.

Irrational and/or Unexplained Fears

Sometimes we are afraid for a reason. If we have past history with a painful event, even something as simple as hitting our thumb with a hammer, the next time we hold a nail, we might be afraid it will happen again. Someone who was once trapped in an elevator for a day might fear enclosed spaces. A person who almost drowned might have a fear of water. In such events, this is normal and is a healthy protective mechanism signaling that we are engaging in the same risky behavior as before. In the case of the hammer, this very rational fear tells us that we might meet with a painful thumb yet again. On the other hand, we all have fears that have no basis in life experience. Whenever we experience irrational fear, we need to discern whether we are picking up a spiritual reality, a spiritual entity causing that fear that's present, or whether it is, indeed, irrational. If the fear has no basis in our experience with no psychic threat, then it is most likely one of our parts experiencing that fear that travels through the bond to our core self. I should mention that even rational fears can receive inner healing, but they are less likely to come from another part, or at least not exclusively from another part.

Stubborn or Perpetual Emotional Problems

When we have already gone through emotional healing for a problem, forgiven everyone and their neighbor's aunt, renounced everything short of life itself, and cast out every demon we could think of (including a few we made up just in case), but we still are not finding emotional relief, the problem might be a fragment. These parts don't respond well to emotional healing we perform on our core self because they are not involved in the healing. We can heal our core all day long, but if the problem doesn't reside in the core, we will need to go elsewhere. Persistent emotional issues can signal the existence of these parts.

Forgetfulness, memory loss, inability to remember certain events, and/or losing blocks of time are major indicators that we have hidden parts. Being unable to remember an entire period of life might indicate a fragment is holding the memories from that time due to a hidden emotional trauma.

Chapter 6: Seneca

Physical Manifestations of

Emotional Trauma

Many of us are beginning to realize that when we pray and command physical healing to manifest to no avail, emotional healing often has to happen first. I believe this is particularly true with chronic disease or illness. If you are doing everything you know to do and have tried everything possible to heal, an emotional root might be the culprit.

In my work, I have begun to notice "trends" among people with various conditions, and I've also dug into research linking negative emotional states and chronic physical conditions.

Many verses in the Bible address the mind/body or spirit/body connection. I've observed many times that by healing the emotions, physical issues lessen or disappear. I'm on a path of learning what connects to what as I frequently have people come to me who do not want to talk about their emotions, only their chronic physical issues. I have had to learn to reverse engineer the healing process by asking them to confirm what I suspect happened to them as an emotional trauma by the physical complaints they have. We then work with flower essences that target that particular wound.

I have been trained in a method called Splankna that works a little differently. While I do not currently practice this method, it involves finding the place in the body where the emotions become stuck after the trauma. This method involves holding meridian points while connecting with but not necessarily reliving specific emotions. Combining this with prayer and forgiveness, it helps discharge the trapped emotions from that part of the body. This process allows the body the opportunity to recover on its own. You can locate a local practitioner online at www.splankna.com.

Since this book is about trauma, I'm going to cover a broad overview of the subject and discuss just a few of the types of issues common to those with emotional trauma.

A Broken Spirit

Many problems with the lymphatic system and immune function are related to trauma. "A merry heart does good like a medicine, but a broken spirit dries up the bones" Proverbs 17:22.

We all know that laughter is the best medicine, and on one level, we accept this part of the verse as true even if we don't have complete understanding of it. But what does it mean to have a broken spirit? This sounds like a figure of speech, right? It's a somewhat controversial conversation, but several of us see value and fruit from ministering to the spirit, not just to the soul or body.

And what about dried-up bones? You may remember that bones are full of two kinds of marrow: red and yellow. Red blood cells, white blood cells, and platelets are formed in the red bone marrow while the yellow produces fat, cartilage, and bone (Tortora 172).

Children have entirely red bone marrow until around the age of seven (Bone). At that point, they start to develop some yellow marrow. This is around the same age that some believe the ability to create your first alter is either no longer possible or highly unlikely. I don't have a dog in that hunt, but it is an interesting coincidence— or perhaps not a coincidence at all.

Let's break this all down. Red blood cells transport oxygen around the body. White blood cells fight infection and disease. Platelets help your blood to clot properly after you cut yourself. I mainly want to discuss the types of white blood cells.

Lymphocytes fight viral infections and send signals to other cells to attack foreign invaders. They modulate nearly all aspects of immune function. Monocytes move into tissues and mature into larger cells called macrophages. Their job is to eat bacteria, fungi, dead cells, and foreign matter. Granulocytes are also infection fighters, and eosinophils attack parasites. Basophils also fight parasites, even external ones such as ticks, and contain histamine and heparin, and are involved in our allergic responses (Tortora 676-678).

Trauma, whether emotional or physical, produces a physiological fight or flight. Cortisol is one of the adrenal hormones necessary to maintain your body's homeostasis. Often called the "stress hormone," it plays a part in this fight-or-flight response, and when it is present long term in high levels, it destroys your immune system.

Catching a little cold once in a while doesn't mean you have a broken spirit. However, having severe immunological issues might. You can see how emotional trauma might lead to a depressed immune system.

Job 17:1 tells us, "My spirit is broken, my days are extinguished, the grave is ready for me."

There's actually a medical condition related to immunodeficiency called Job's Syndrome. Characteristics are eczema, facial and dental abnormalities, and recurrent staph, candida, and pneumonia infections.

Chronic Pain

The American Chronic Pain Association defines chronic pain as any pain that persists beyond the point of a normal healing process (Chronic). This can stem from old injuries, but many people suffering with chronic pain have no history of injury. People with fibromyalgia, migraines, and chronic musculoskeletal pain tend to carry with them a greater history of emotional trauma than those without these kinds of issues. Emotional pain that goes unacknowledged often turns into physical pain.

I work with flower essences, which theoretically have no direct effect on the physical body whatsoever, yet I have a blend called "Align" for back problems that gives most people positive results. This is because the flower essences address the emotional states responsible for their pain.

For those suffering with chronic pain as a result of a legitimate accident, such as a car crash, with no emotional roots, you might have other reasons why you do not heal. These can vary from emotional trauma finding your weak spot to a spirit of trauma that simply needs casting out to a nervous system issue—but even that problem might have an underlying emotional root.

When we experience a traumatic event, our sympathetic nervous system—the fight-or-flight response—kicks in. Sometimes, we have trouble moving back into parasympathetic or relaxed, at-rest responses after the event is over. This is particularly true if events in our lives constantly retrigger us to make us believe that we are in danger, such as getting in a car after the accident. Staying in a fight-or-flight state causes muscle tension and constriction that over time, means the muscle becomes fatigued, causing pain. While this example of trauma is not generally linked to fragmentation, it still has emotional roots that need healing.

A Testimony of Back Pain Being Healed Along with Fragmentation

"My friends have been raving about Seneca's essences. I finally gave in and asked her to send me a sample. Since I've been on a journey to learn about and receive my own emotional healing, I asked if I could try an experimental essence called "Fragment Finder."

The first night I took "Fragment Finder," I had a dream where different aliases and personas I had used during my lifetime were being revealed. (Aliases and personas are essentially alters.)

I've been suffering from chronic back pain, a combination of stiffness and dull pain that's the most painful in the morning. I've lived with it virtually every day for at least ten years. I've received prayer for it many times, but nothing has relieved it. However, about six months ago, I was seen by a doctor who said I have changes in my x-ray consistent with arthritis.

The morning after I began taking "Fragment Finder," I awoke for the first time in years without any pain or stiffness. The same thing happened the next day and then on the third day. It wasn't until the third day that it dawned on me my usual pain and stiffness was gone.

On the fourth day that I was taking the essence, I had an unscheduled emotional healing session with Matt Evans. He happened to call me up, and we worked on my emotional healing for two hours over the phone. In the session, we found one major and two minor alters that were healed and integrated. A number of fragments were also healed and integrated. It's possible this could have been done without the essence, but I want to report what happened as completely as I can while I was taking it.

Last, I've been dreaming regularly since 2008. I typically have dreams about seven nights out of ten. On the nights when I have a dream, 99 percent of the time, I only have one dream. Since taking "Fragment Finder," I'm now having two dreams most nights when I dream, and last night, I had so many dreams that I could not count or journal them all.

I once was a skeptic, but now I'm a believer. I'll be using Seneca's essences from now on. -Praying Medic

Autoimmune Diseases

The correlation between early childhood trauma and autoimmune disease is astounding, especially for women. In dealing with people in my day-to-day life, I noticed this link myself, and after hearing from others in different healing modalities who had also seen the correlation, I went digging for the proof. I found a study supporting my findings published by the American Psychosomatic Society (Dube). This study researched the possible link between the scores of each of 15,357 participants with Adverse Childhood Experience (ACE) and their medical records. The results were staggering.

The link between childhood trauma and later developing an autoimmune condition is comparable to the link between a fast-food diet and obesity or between alcoholism and liver failure.

For every ACE a person has, the likelihood of a first hospitalization with any autoimmune disease increased 20 percent for women and 10 percent for men. In other words, a woman with three adverse childhood experiences is 60 percent more likely to be hospitalized with an autoimmune condition than a woman with no adverse childhood experiences.

The types of ACEs include "childhood physical, emotional, or sexual abuse; witnessing domestic violence; growing up with household substance abuse, mental illness, parental divorce, and/or an incarcerated household member (Dube).

Where to Begin

Now that we know that negative emotions and traumatic experiences can cause illness and disease, we need to know what to do about them. In the next section of this book, we'll explore some exercises for healing memories and fragments. In addition, the Lord has led me to develop a line of flower essences that are designed to help each individual release the energy of these negative emotions, a process I explain in greater detail in my book, *Flower Power: Essences That Heal.*

This is just one of many methods for releasing emotional trauma. However you do it, a crucial part of one's healing journey is to begin releasing negative emotions.

If you aren't sure where to start, begin by making a list of everyone in your life you need to forgive and those you need to ask forgiveness from. Ask Holy Spirit to show you those that you might have forgotten. Jesus told his disciples in John 20:23 that "If you forgive the sins of any, their sins have been forgiven them; if you retain the sins of any, they have been retained."

This has major implications for how we can keep others emotionally captive through unforgiveness, but it also means that we are bound as well. Jesus clearly stated in Matthew 7:2 that "For in the way you judge, you will be judged; and by your standard of measure, it will be measured to you."

If we do not forgive others, we hold onto the negative emotions of those situations, and our bodies reap the damage. On the other hand, as we forgive others, we not only set them free, we set ourselves free—and from time to time, we might notice that joint pain, arthritis, low back pain, and other physical problems either lessen or disappear entirely.

Whether dealing with forgiveness or other emotional issues, resolving them is a major key to physical healing. If you have had everyone who knows Jesus's cousin's friend's great-great grandson lay hands on you and you still haven't been healed of a physical problem, consider switching your focus to the realm of emotions. While we all came to it individually, all of the coauthors of this book have found that dealing with emotions works very effectively in healing prayer. If you have struggled with chronic pain for years and are even considering giving up on healing because of unanswered prayer, let me encourage you to keep pressing on. There is hope for a solution, and emotional healing is probably the answer you have been seeking.

Chapter 7: Matt

Where Do All These Parts

Come From?

Trauma at an early age seems likely to cause the development of more heavily fractured parts. Some of the most heavily fractured people I've worked with were test-tube babies or those whose parents were mentally ill or extremely violent and abusive. Some have been abused in cults from an early age. On the other hand, many who have not been through such difficult childhoods also have many parts that need serious healing.

I generally see a huge difference in the nature of the parts found among those severely traumatized at the youngest ages when compared with the nature of the parts of those who weren't. Also, the complexity of the system that the parts form tends to differ. Both groups have parts, and though one group seems a bit more like "parts lite," they still have issues that will usually not be healed in any other way except through intentional ministry to this area.

This is similar to healing the sick in a hospital. If you went into the hospital and just wandered around, reading the Bible and worshipping, you would most likely see very few healings. However, if you learned your authority in Christ and how to move in physical healing and intentionally prayed with all the sick people in that hospital, you would see many more healings than you would through an aimless approach that lacks intentional focus. The healing of inner issues works in much the same way. You will accomplish much more with some basic know-how and intentional action as opposed to aimless wandering.

Many like to think that these issues are healing on their own without anybody doing anything about them. We like to think that what the church is doing is working and that the broken are being healed by just following their programs. However, my experience says that this isn't the case.

Instead, I see many Christians remaining wounded and many of them being aggressively persuaded to believe they are completely healed when they aren't. I see a lot of traditionally minded people giving up on real healing and transformation because it just hasn't happened over many years despite doing all the popular "Christian things" the best they knew how.

Many think of fractured parts as only found in the most extreme cases, such as the ritually abused or those diagnosed with Dissociative Identity Disorder (DID). They think that only psychologists can minister to this phenomenon. I've found that not only is this the farthest thing from the truth, but this mentality is directly responsible for leaving multitudes stuck in a place of brokenness. Many stagnate because they don't know how to access or minister to these parts of themselves where their deep woundedness lives.

As I've gained more experience and understanding over the last fifteen-plus years, and as I've prayed with people from many states and countries, I've come to believe that we can find fractured parts in everyone to varying degrees and that healing them is necessary for our own personal progress.

The Body of Christ needs to learn and apply this to the massive numbers of people who so desperately need healing wherever we look. Again, this is a matter of whether we will allow the Lord to continue with that basic aspect of his mission statement from Isaiah 61, which, when well-translated says, "to heal and bind together those who are shattered into many pieces."

Section 2:

How to Get in Touch With and Heal Fractured Parts

Chapter 8:

Using Your Gifts and

Imagination

Michael:

Healing one's parts is easiest when working with a counselor of some kind. However, even if you have a prayer partner or counselor available, a significant benefit of self-healing methods is that you can accelerate the integration process. I personally use the work I do with a counselor as a foundation to pursue further prayer work, primarily involving interactive visualization, on my own.

Visualization techniques might sound like just using your imagination, and in reality they are, but the imagination is the gateway for spiritual engagement. We encounter visions and dreams via the backdrop of the imagination, and visualization can jump-start real-life encounters. Our thoughts guide our spiritual interaction, so a guided visual technique can help us work through emotional issues, integrate various parts, and more.

The actual methods one can use are as varied as spoken languages, but we will share those that we have developed and found helpful. You might use one or more as we have described or use them as a base to develop your own approach. If one plan doesn't work for you, try something else. Whether following these visualizations closely or using them as a guide to find your own methods that work, keep in mind that the goal is freedom, not adherence to a particular methodology or technique.

Seneca:

To build upon what Michael said about imagination, I want to emphasize that it is a gift that God gave you to display information from the spirit. Most of us were taught to disregard these impressions as "that's just my imagination." If you've ever thought this, you'll need to repent and then sanctify your imagination to see and function out of the spirit.

The vast majority of us that have visions don't see them as an altered sense of physical reality with our eyes wide open. Sometimes this is the case, but I mostly see with closed eyes or staring into space while an image similar to a movie plays on the screen of my mind. I can very easily pass this off as "just" my imagination.

Many people have a deep-seated fear of seeing something wrong or evil or of falling into deception. Listen, if you can have a vain imagination, you can have a holy one, too. Turn your heart toward God, and you'll be okay.

Most of us that are grown have to make a point of exercising our imaginations if we want to consistently see in the spirit.

That said, all of the skills and spiritual gifts that you currently have will help you in this arena. The way you have already learned to hear the Lord will translate to listening to your parts. All it takes is a shift in focus and a little practice.

If you are more of a "feeler," then you can simply speak out loud to your parts and sense their reaction to what you've said.

If you see in the spirit, great! If not, that's okay, too, although this book was written by a bunch of visual people, so our examples and exercises have a bent in that direction.

If you are interested in developing that skill further, I have another book that I coauthored with some friends called *Accessing Your Spiritual Inheritance* with a full section on seeing in the spirit.

Any method through which you receive revelation will work. Your experience does not have to look like our experience, and all of your senses are beneficial and useful.

Chapter 9: Seneca

Identifying Parts Through

Dreams

The most common way I become aware of or interact with parts is in dreams. Because our conscious minds have made a point of burying certain emotions and events, our dream life is a prime way for them to come to the surface.

We can either dream from the part's point of view or from our core personality's point of view. Because parts can live in various internal structures, sometimes these will come out via a dream, such as a house that isn't your actual house, castle, dungeon, cave or cavern, underground places, city, or a magical place. These types of constructs are real in another dimension and therefore, do not necessarily need to be symbolically interpreted.

The less obvious situations are when the core self is dreaming, and we are interacting with one or more of our fragments in a dream. We tend to see them as friends, helpers, people you sense but don't see, or if you see them, they have some similarity to you or your circumstance.

Many Christian dream interpretation resources state that the unknown people that you can't see are angels, which can be true. However, I'm here to a throw a wrench into that generalization and say that isn't always the case. Many parts are created to protect you so that they can appear in very similar dream circumstances, much like angels. However, parts tend to be more alarmist and are not known for accurate judgment in situations.

That friend in your dream might also represent a piece of you rather than the actual person. I have dreams of vague friends, people I don't know but who are my friend in the dream, as well as existing friends who show up in dreams. Many times, the meaning of their name indicates their purpose. For instance, if I'm in a situation where my friend Mary and I are fighting with my mother over something, I might look up the meaning of Mary, see that it means 'bitter,' and realize that I have a part that's formed around bitterness. Other times, the meaning might relate to the attributes or the occupation of that friend.

You will almost always experience some tip off if you know to look for it to determine if that other person in your dream is a part. The most obvious is when it's another you. I've never been so lucky as to have such a blatant experience, but a couple of my friends have. I have had a dream where an anonymous "friend" and I were dressed alike in layered clothing. Then, a trigger situation happened, and we split up.

You can also have multiple fragments in a dream. Here's an example. In one of my dreams, my trigger situation comes up. This fragment's MO is always to hide. I want to disappear, fade away, or not exist. But instead, I am sitting down to eat at this table, which I know is 2,000 years old. I'm honored and can feel the worn texture of the surface. I remember thinking, "Man, this table has seen some stuff!" The "stuff" represents everybody's issues. I knew there was an energetic record of all of it.

Others come and sit down with me on the same side, and I believe that they are fragments, less formed ones that are in some way attached to this situation. These fragments were very thin, almost 2D. The person who hurt me came, sat down with food, and we had a conversation. I then realized I might have misread the situation. I was still a little skeptical, but then, I realized that this was the Last Supper table; this was communion, the meal that heals, and all of this was about to go to the cross. This entire scenario played out in slow motion over the next few days.

Another clue for me has been when I'm trying to figure out someone's identity in the dream. Activity will be going on, and I keep looking at the person and trying to get them to tell me who they are. Sometimes I get names; mostly, I get weird answers. I have permission to share an example dream snippet from a client with you. It seems to go nicely with Sam's "storage cubby" analogy in Chapter 1, which is that some parts are merely places where we stuff emotions that we can't deal with, rather than having fully formed alternate personalities.

Cheryl's Dream

Cheryl's dream follows:

On a table were these oddly shaped boxes. I asked them their names. One responded, "'I am the one that can't seem to love me for who I am." I didn't catch the name of the other one, but it became a person, and I had it bound so that it couldn't harm me. The person was a young girl in a dress that was rather worn with her hair in a pixie cut. I had hair like that from age eight to ten.

65

If you do not see a resolution in the dream itself in any of your dream scenarios, consider that your cue to intentionally address the situation via techniques in this book.

Here's one of my dreams from the first night I took the "Fragment Finder" flower essence.

There were two different scenario dreams. In the first, I was outside a church; in the second, I was at some Christian event. In the first, I saw a sign on the outside of a church rejecting a certain man named Francis. All of the reasons for rejecting him, including judgmental comments, were written for all to see with an attached note that said not to remove the list. Both scenarios involved a public shaming and rejection. I was angry at this and thought that it was gossip and slander. I knew I could not stay mad and that I had to forgive. I went upstairs to my old room in mom's house. I was younger at this point in the dream, and in the room across the hall was the boy, Francis, who had been kicked out. I went and sat down on the floor in my messy room. I watched as he came into the hallway between our rooms and lay on the floor, wanting to be closer to me.

Since I am purposely taking "Fragment Finder," and because the above scenario is extremely close to home emotionally speaking, I know this is a dream with content to show me how to heal. Interestingly, Francis is a family name, so this might have a generational aspect to it as my family has never done well in the organized church. Here, "Francis" wants to connect with me, so I need to employ some of the techniques in this book as well as forgive and let go of anger.

Tammy's Dream

Let's look at a dream scenario where the fragment is not ready yet:

I was in a room, perhaps a hospital room, talking with some others, but I didn't know who they were. My sister, who I have not had a relationship with for a couple years, walks in. She is looking at me and walks directly to me with her hand held out. She is holding a key chain with many, many keys on it. I see a car key and realize that these are all of her keys: to her house and personal items, etc. She hands the key to me and turns to walk away.

I am overwhelmed that she is giving me these keys. I ask, "What are these?" I know they mean that she has given me access back into her life, but I want to hear her say it.

I follow her outside, still asking, "What are these?" She turns to me, and I try to hug her. She answers, "Not yet." Her heart isn't quite ready yet.

My sister is known for holding in her feelings to the point that she has suffered physically, especially in the past few years, requiring surgeries and iron infusions for the havoc in her stomach and her soul. This is how I recognized that she was representing those parts of me that would not give up their pain.

I had this dream at a time when many emotional wounds were beginning to surface, and it was time to heal from issues that I had been carrying most of my life.

Here's the sequel to that dream a couple months later:

At a house, my sister comes over and is talking to me, which amazes me. Overwhelmed with emotions, I say, "I wish I could talk to you on the phone."

She responds, "No, I'm not ready for that, but we can talk now." She begins opening up more.

Months later, Tammy had another dream where her sister asked her to come and clean out her house. House cleaning typically indicates deliverance.

Here is another dream of mine although I'm not sure what part this referenced. It was during a period where I was interacting with other people's fragments in dreams so it might have been mine, or it might not have. It also might have been purely a teaching dream.

I was watching someone's fragment go through a constant process of torment. I watched her move through these different dimensions in the spirit to escape the enemy's involvement. The closer dimensions, and I don't know that 'closer' is the right word, were areas in the spirit realm that still had a lot of demonic involvement. She retreated to a safer and deeper place and then came back out until she couldn't take any more, once again retreating into another dimension. I then saw her go through all of the layers, and I knew that if she went to the last one, she could not go back, and she would cease to exist on earth. She did just that and went right into Jesus' arms and melded into him. He was smiling; I was pretty upset. I was happy for her, yet the thought of ceasing to exist on earth bothered me.

What happens to the person who then has a piece missing? This was not part of my current grid for how integration worked. My view was that it was self-contained. I had never considered that parts could integrate with Jesus.

I stewed over this for several days until I had an answer. This came via an offhand remark from someone that when you become one with Jesus, you become a new creation. This sparked other verses in a chain reaction related to our union with Christ and how ceasing to exist on earth means that part of you is seated in heavenly places and ruling from an entirely different position rather than as a trapped fragment. You haven't lost anything—quite the opposite. For a person whose primary personality is not in union with Christ, that part is kept safe, and the person becomes whole when they eventually make that decision. This is a more dramatic healing for them. In the meantime, the enemy has no access to that previously wounded part.

I mentioned that this came during a time of interacting with parts belonging to others during my dreams. I'll expand a little more on that.

When I go to bed, I first open up a portal if one isn't there already. I declare it off limits to any of the demonic realms and state that it is only for angels, Holy Spirit, and those ministering by Holy Spirit. I then speak to my spirit and release it to go and minister to others under the tutelage of Holy Spirit while I sleep.

The reason I don't stop with only allowing angels and Holy Spirit through the portal is that if I'm out and about helping others, I figure I should be open to reciprocity. Healings, impartations, people prophesying to me, and deliverances happen in my dreams. The early hours of my nights seem to be when I act on the behalf of others, while the middle appears to be when I'm the recipient, and closer to morning seems to be the more informative type of dreams. Now that I've said this, everything will probably change!

The first time I intentionally spoke the above prayer, I saw something almost exactly like Jacob's ladder descending through a rectangular portal. The next day, I was reading some Jewish interpretations of Genesis 28 about how Jacob was quite busy serving God in his sleep; he went up to the heavenly academy at night and studied the Torah, and his first revelation that we could accomplish much in our sleep was at Bethel. While I cannot now recall the name of the text I read this in, and while this was clearly extra-biblical information, it was interesting nonetheless.

Here's an example of how that interaction works. I was in a dream once, sitting across the table from Michael, the coauthor. In the dream, I know it is not actually him, but rather a fragment-version of him, and no one else seems to pick up on this. The dream is as follows:

I say, "Hello, who are you?" The fragment is not sure and is confused about where he is and why. I hold out my hand and introduce myself. I tell him that I might have an idea of what is happening here. I ask him if he knows who Michael is. He stated he thought that the name sounded familiar, but he wasn't sure why or how. I explained the process of dissociation and asked this part if he could forgive Michael for having him carry the pain. He asked a couple clarifying questions, and we discussed the subject further. He decided to forgive. Then, I asked him if he knew Jesus Christ, at which point I was yanked backward out of my chair, and that was the end of the dream.

Interestingly enough, prior to having that dream, Michael had a series of fragment-dreams all in one night, the very first night he used one of the main components of the "Fragment Finder" essence. Each dream depicted a fragment either coming to terms with his reality and experiences or fighting dark forces that were out to harm them. In one dream, the fragment was explaining to a group of people that he only had two weeks' worth of memories but that he knew all sorts of factual and scientific information due to sharing memories with other versions of himself that existed in other dimensions. What was fascinating about this particular dream was that the fragment was conscious that he had other counterparts in other dimensions as well as the fact that these parts were able to share knowledge and information.

Chapter 10: Matt

Basics of How I Minister to Parts

The basic idea behind what I typically do is to encourage the parts to personally communicate with the Lord and to allow Him to do the heavy lifting of counseling and healing them directly. I rely on the Lord, directly or through my own prayer of faith, to miraculously remove the woundedness from the parts before integrating them.

You can connect with the fractured parts in several ways to begin communicating with them so that you can invite the Lord to minister to them and bring healing.

- Some people call them "up" or to the surface of a person's consciousness to actually "switch" or take control of the body. While some people find success with this approach, I prefer to use other methods when possible. From here, you can have a conversation with a fractured part just as with the normal personality of the one you are ministering to as it speaks through their vocal cords. Depending on how severely fractured a person is, they might experience a subtle or drastic shift take place, such as a headache during the switching.

- Rather than having people "switch," I typically like to talk to people's parts out loud—they can usually hear you—and ask them to put thoughts and pictures in the person's mind and feelings into their emotional awareness.

  This is just as if the person was listening to the Lord, but instead, they are listening to a part of themselves. Many times, this seems to be easier on the person receiving ministry. Also, this allows them to communicate with and walk their own parts through healing when nobody is around to help.

- Another way is to perceive the parts in the spirit: for instance, to see them in vision form and to go to them "in the spirit," bringing the Lord with you. This way, you can communicate with them in the spiritual realm without needing to physically speak out loud. You can introduce them to Jesus, releasing Him to minister to them however He wants to.

As you watch the Lord begin to minister, trust Him to accomplish the first thing He is doing. Then, wait for Him to show you what's next, watch Him do that, and so on. You might recognize the part receiving various kinds of help, which is often different every time, until the part seems to disappear, becoming integrated into the rest of the person.

A First Step

In any of those three approaches, it can be very helpful to start by binding up and restraining the demonic from hindering ministry in any way and specifically binding up and keeping the demonic from manipulating or controlling any part of the person, causing them to impede or block ministry.

The enemy will often use parts over which he has control, especially Protectors, to stand in the way of healing. Yes, different parts tend to have different jobs: Protectors, helpers, carriers of pain, ones to function in the outside world, etc. This often looks like sudden mental distractions, outbursts of anger, feelings of numbness or of being overwhelmed, theological arguments, etc. These activities are often not the person's true intention or anything they can control but are a matter of their parts forced into behaving this way by the demonic. These behaviors stop immediately when the enemy is restrained from controlling or manipulating the parts.

Onto the ABCs

- Discern the parts and listen to them. Ask for any of the following: an image of what they look like, what condition they are in, what they are carrying, and what is around them. Ask them to share anything on their heart, their emotions, anything they wish to say, etc.

- Bring Jesus or another member of the Trinity to the part/s by faith and help them begin a relationship with Him. He might need to reveal Himself to them a little at a time, explain something to them, heal them from something small, or give them gifts or food, etc., to help them start to trust Him. Just ask Him to minister to them however He wants to and work with the parts to help them receive from Him.

- Sometimes, false "Jesuses" might need to be exposed and removed before the parts can come into relationship with the real Jesus. This is often the case with religious backgrounds or heritages. Have the parts make sure to look into Jesus' eyes to check whether everything they see is good and whether they see love. If they don't see love or if they see any negative qualities in the eyes, they aren't seeing Jesus but a religious spirit.

You don't want a demon posing as Jesus ministering to the parts as this might hurt them. You can use your authority in Christ to expose the tricksters and then ask for permission from the parts to remove them. As you lead the parts in renouncing agreements with religious spirits and in eliminating all the counterfeits, you will soon find the true Jesus showing up with love in His eyes.

- Make sure that all the parts receive Jesus as their Lord and Savior. Simply ask them if they want to do this. If they answer, "Yes," consider it done. If they aren't ready for this, He can just reveal Himself to them a little at a time, maybe from a distance, and minister to them at whatever level they are comfortable with until they become ready for more.

- Once the part is in a relationship with Jesus, seek the part's permission to let the Lord remove any anger, unforgiveness, shame, trauma, negative emotions, demonic, or any problem issues. He can take these away instantly and miraculously. If they experience any hang up during this process or if the parts object to letting Jesus do this for any reason, He can work with them to resolve this if they are willing to let Him talk to them. If they have a "Jesus" who can't or won't do these things, it is a false Jesus and indicates a need to break an agreement with a religious or occult spirit.

- Overt agreements with the demonic, issues of hatred/anger/resentment/unforgiveness, and issues of shame often need to be resolved early on since these things can prevent other areas of woundedness from being healed. If you are finding that emotions such as sorrow, rejection, or fear just aren't leaving, you might look for anger and shame as likely culprits locking the pain in place.

The parts' clothes often need to be changed from colored to white, representing purity in the spiritual realm. This will happen as all their issues are resolved, and colored clothes typically represent unresolved problems. The parts might also need to be taken out of a bad place, such as a dark cave or a dungeon filled with demons, etc., and moved to a better, safer place to finish receiving ministry.

- After they are healed up, they might go somewhere with Jesus to take a break for a while before receiving more healing another day, or they might help with finding and communicating to or for other parts or groups of parts so that the Lord can continue healing all of them in the same way. They might be ready for integration into the whole person. Have them ask the Lord if they are ready to be integrated and to follow Him into the light to be integrated if He says yes.

This is all done from a place of listening and discerning the parts just as if you were listening to the Lord rather than from a place of exploring memories and reliving emotional pain. This is a totally different approach than secular trauma processing. The Lord miraculously takes away the pain as the parts simply give Him permission to do so as opposed to feeling the pain all over again and processing through it.

Chapter 11: Diane

My Approach to Healing

Fragments

When helping a client with an issue from a young age, I will often have them look for an inner child, a fragment of themselves. I will teach them what they're looking for and ask them, "Who's speaking in there?" I will tell them to look inside to see who is telling them a lie or who has an issue. Usually, they will see the child in their mind's eye, or sometimes they will hear the child speak. Those who have shut off their imagination because it is scary to them will tend to be the ones who will hear instead of see.

I will often discern the age of the child for confirmation, which is the age when the trauma occurred. I have them explore how the child looks, what they're wearing, what's going on, how they feel, and have the child tell the person their story. I want the person talking to the child rather than me because I want the person's will involved. I want them to tell the child that God is safe, etc. Then, whenever the child is ready to hear from God, I invite Him in to speak. I let Jesus heal the child as He wants to, and I ask the person to report what He is doing.

Talk to the fragment and let them know that you are happy they are there, that it's okay that they are there. You might say, "I realize that you are carrying memory and woundedness that is stuck there, and I want to help get you unstuck." Let them know that God knows that they are there and that He is happy about it, that He cares. Realize that as you are talking, this fragment is hearing you. I address that fact and let the child/children know that I'm glad that they can hear me, and I share what I want them to understand.

This part is often exactly who you were at that age: saved, unsaved, religiously indoctrinated, etc. Listen to Holy Spirit and relay what to say next to the child, for example, "God isn't mad at you, etc." Then, listen as this fragment begins to talk and to share what's on their heart.

Ask the child questions about what they're feeling. Do they feel depressed, unclean, mad? I'm looking for the ungodly belief/s that the fragment has accepted. You are evangelizing the child, telling them how great and loving God is, how He loves them right where they're at, and how He is glad they're there. You are giving them a positive view of God and a positive view of how God sees them.

When they are ready, introduce them to the Lord so that they can hear Him. Ask them, "Is it okay if the Lord comes and talks to you about or heals those issues? Do you want to talk to the Lord about that and see what He has to say?" I want them to see the Lord. What the Lord does is always different and always brings healing.

If you feel that a demon is present, look on the back of the fragment to see if something is attached to the back. I've had different people tell me that there were iron spikes in the child's back, stripes on the back, dark spots, beings attached, etc. In each of these cases, I've had the Spirit of the true Lord Jesus Christ remove what was on the child's back. He does so immediately without any interference from the demons. It's usually quick and completely supernatural!

Ask the Lord if they have anything else to deal with or if He wants to say anything. Pay attention to what they are wearing. Girls usually wear dresses. If the girls are wearing overalls or pants to begin with, they likely are struggling with homosexuality, rejecting their femininity, or the abuse might have involved the overalls or pants. Clothing always seems to end up in all white as a result of dealing with their issues. Often, the child will be spontaneously integrated into the core person as Jesus is working or as He finishes up healing.

Check the child's clothing again. If the issues are addressed, the child will usually be dressed in all white. If other colors are present, this often represents a problem, and you will want to ask the Lord what He intends to do for the child next. He also might give them colored clothes for a purpose, but most of the time, the clothing will be all white.

One of my favorite testimonies of the healing of fragments is also a story that I consider to be a textbook case:

It was only our second healing session. Shannon had been a victim of severe abuse all her life. Beatings, molestations, rape, addictions, verbal abuse—she had experienced it all. She freely admitted to drug and alcohol addictions since the age of five. I asked her if we could deal with some fragments and explained to her what they were.

She was very tentative. The thought of fragments was very strange and completely out of her comfort zone. She was a new believer in the Lord, and these concepts just sounded a bit too out there, but she decided to give it a try.

I told her that I could see the fragments, so if she couldn't, that was okay. We started praying, and as soon as I said that I could see the fragment, she told me she could see it as well. She then mostly took over from there with just a little guidance from me. She saw what the fragment was carrying. Three more of them showed up, and she asked Jesus to come and heal them.

She saw a video replay, which she seemed to be watching from the back of the room, of one of the instances of abuse. As she watched this replay, she also saw the Lord come into the situation and protect her, comforting her. No one else had protected her. She saw Jesus heal the fragment that had been stuck in this memory. Then, she saw the Lord take all four of the fragments to a new place.

The new place she saw is a place I believe that we all have within us—our own "Garden of Eden"—a beautiful place that might be a garden, an ocean, a forest, or even a lake. These locations might even change when you go another time.

The Lord dwells in this place, and you can be with Him at any point, just as Adam and Eve were before the fall. Many times, people have told me that angels and Jesus were there to play with the children. It is a beautiful place for fragments that have been kept in darkness, bright and sunny with glorious vistas. I always think of the line that makes up the title of the Big Daddy Weave song titled , "Dancing with My Father God in Fields of Grace" when the Lord takes the fragments there.

Often, the child/fragment will spontaneously integrate into the core person as Jesus is working with him/her. If they don't integrate, then don't worry about it. You might run into this fractured part again, or it might integrate without you knowing about it.

If the person cannot see or hear the fragment for themselves, I will go and talk to the fragments in the spirit realm. I will find the fragment and describe it to the person. Usually, they can confirm that what I'm seeing is accurate either because they have the tendency I'm describing or they remember the event that I'm relating. I speak to the fragment and introduce it to the Lord. He talks to the fragment and heals it every time.

Sometimes, the fragment has other fragments connected to it. I have commonly seen from three to more than twenty fragments related to one incident. The Lord heals them corporately yet one by one. To elaborate, I introduce the Lord to them corporately, and He heals them at the same time, but one by one since He is not limited to just talking to one at a time. I have seen more than 100 fragments healed at once.

One important fact about fragments—since they have their own will, I can travel in the spirit and heal the fragment of someone who isn't open to ministry. As long as the fragment is okay with receiving prayer, the Lord will come and heal them. Praying for fragments is quite useful when praying for spouses who aren't open to the Lord as well as praying for children and even parents.

I discovered this when a friend was suffering emotional abuse at the hands of her husband. I went into the spirit realm and saw a fragment that was controlling him. As I asked the Lord to go to the fragment, I saw that fragment give his pain and sorrow to the Lord and receive healing. My friend reported that the emotional abuse ceased immediately after I prayed. I have prayed for fragments of people who did not ask for ministry a number of times now with reported success.

A typical session looks like Nicole's. She was a daddy's girl who loved her dad and thought the world of him. However, her father died in a car accident when Nicole was only eleven years old. A fragment broke off in her at the time to hold the grief, sorrow, and pain of her dad's death.

To this fragment, her dad had just died, and the shock of his death was fresh every day. This child also blamed God for her father's death. Even though Nicole knew that a drunk driver was to blame and not God, the child fragment felt that God should have protected her dad's life.

We asked the fragment if it was okay to ask God why He didn't protect her father's life. This took a little encouragement and reassurance that God wasn't mad at her before she was willing to ask Him (That is normal.). She asked the Lord, and He responded to her quickly with a surprising answer.

He showed her that it wasn't her fault. Unknown to me, eleven-year-old Nicole had delayed her father from leaving by asking him to fix one of her toys. In her subconscious, she had blamed herself because he was in that place at that time. If she hadn't asked him to fix her toy, he wouldn't have been hit by the drunk driver. Once the Lord healed this issue, the fragment was able to let go of the trauma, grief, sorrow, and pain and be completely healed.

Many times when dealing with fragments, the Lord heals one child, and then another one speaks up because it wants to be healed as well. You might have three or more fragments healed in one session. Some of them are connected by the same or a similar memory while some don't seem to be connected at all.

I was once ministering to a woman, and as we healed one fragment from the pain of childhood sexual abuse, another one spoke up. If I hadn't been sure that God had healed the first fragment, I would have thought it was the same one. The first child carried the pain, and this one took the shame of the abuse. We had the Lord minister to it, bringing it forward into His light. (Shame hides, so this one was hiding inside.)

As His light shone upon the child, the dress this fragment was wearing turned from dirty black into pure white. God took away the shame and brought a new purity to her. Immediately, a voice spoke up in this woman's mind, "Me, too!" Another fragment was jumping out of the shadows. As we introduced her to the Lord, he healed her, and we didn't even find out specifics because the healing happened so quickly. That one wanted to heal and was already prepared to jump into her Father's arms.

After this, I spoke to her system and asked if there was anyone else who was ready for God's healing. We waited for about thirty seconds and heard nothing. I started to pray to seal what God had done and to affirm the client when she said to me, "Wait a minute. I have this thought going around in my brain, and it just won't quit." I asked her to tell me about the thought. She replied, "Not safe. It's going to happen again." This fragment carried fear.

I spoke to her and let her know that God could keep her safe. That didn't work, though. After all, God didn't keep her safe from the abuse she suffered. To the fragment, her experience outweighed anything I said on the matter.

I knew that I couldn't talk her into it, so I did what I should have from the beginning. I asked her if we could ask Jesus about all this and let Him explain why He didn't keep her safe. She agreed to that, so she asked Jesus about it.

He answered her in such a gentle and kind manner. He showed her that he couldn't stop people from doing evil things because they had the freedom to sin, but He showed her that He went through the abuse with her and held her the entire time. He showed her that while her body was being abused, he was holding her soul/spirit in His arms, keeping her safe. This brought healing to her fragment because now she felt safe. No other fragment spoke up after that, allowing us to seal and affirm what the Lord had done for her.

I prayed for another woman who felt she was still in love with an old boyfriend. He had dumped her, and she just couldn't let go. Soul/spirit ties had been broken, yet her love for him remained. We dealt with a fragment within her who was still connected to this old boyfriend. The fragment was there because of a trauma the two of them had experienced together. Once this fragment was healed, the love for her former boyfriend was gone. She saw him after that, and she no longer felt love for him.

Letting go of former lovers is a common problem. I have prayed for numerous women who could not let go of abusive husbands or boyfriends. Healing the fragment was the answer in this instance. Other issues can cause feelings of continued connection as well. She might have a mothering part of her that sees the little boy in him and believes in him. It might be tricky to find healing as a demon almost always enforces these beliefs. Set aside the demon until the mothering part is delivered from this belief, then evict the demon afterward. Victim mentality and patterns of abuse might also be present. Be sure to address them as well.

Traveling in the Spirit Approach

As I worked with fragments and in healing the human spirit, I noticed that I was seeing these fragments in the spirit as I prayed with people. I could see the fragments, and I could also see the Lord healing them.

I decided to minister to these fragments without the person seeing them to find out if that worked. It did. This has made ministry so much easier. Sometimes both of us see the same thing happening, and sometimes the Lord has the person see the details of what is happening while I see it from a distance.

I will share a few examples of this. Once, I prayed with Sarah, a thirty-year-old hair stylist who had begun having nightmares and trouble sleeping. As I looked into the spirit realm, I saw a fragment that was carrying a burden. As I invited Jesus to her, I saw Jesus introduce Himself and then ask her if she was willing to give the burden to Him.

84

She wasn't willing at first. She grabbed a hold of it tighter and shook her head no. I saw Jesus talking to her. I didn't know what He was saying, but on the other hand, Sarah did. As I was describing out loud what I was seeing, she told me that Jesus was saying that she could trust Him to carry that burden for her. He was bigger and stronger and much more capable of carrying it.

As Sarah was telling me this, I saw the fragment release the burden to the Lord and be completely healed. Jesus took the fragment to a new place.

Although I was seeing what was happening in the spirit, Sarah not only saw it, but she saw it more clearly, and she knew what Jesus was saying to her fragment. This was because she was able to connect with the fragment and experience what the fragment experienced as the Lord healed it. This is my favorite way of dealing with the fragments. It doesn't always happen this way, but I trust God that when it doesn't, it doesn't need to.

An example of when events unfolded differently is Paula's story. Paula fought the healing process. She wanted healing, but her control and stubbornness hindered her from progressing quickly. No matter what I did to try and connect her to her fragments, the connection was tenuous and lasted briefly. She only had partial memories and was never able to connect the child to the Lord. She never saw or heard anything when she tried to connect the Lord and her fragments, although she has multiple testimonies of hearing God clearly.

One day, I saw her fragment in the spirit, and instead of trying to connect Paula with the child, I just started telling Paula what I saw happening. I told her that the fragment was afraid of God because she felt responsible for the abuse.

When I asked the Lord to come to her and reveal the lie, I let Paula know what God was saying and how the child was responding to Him. The child allowed the Lord to come and heal her, and Paula felt the difference immediately.

Paula had a habit of blaming herself for every little thing that went wrong; it was always her fault. After the fragment was healed, that very same day, one of her kids tripped over a toy and bit their lip as they fell to the floor, crying. Paula went and comforted her child. Instead of blaming herself and telling herself that she should have already picked up that toy and put it away, she realized that the incident was merely an accident and was normal with no need to place blame on anyone. She was free.

Chapter 12: Sam

Storage Cubby Cleansing

This exercise works especially well during triggered moments or if you are only able to identify strong emotions or painful memories. Stay flexible and listen to Jesus. You don't have to be able to see, and if you do see, you don't have to see everything unfold as if it were a movie. Sometimes, you hear more than you see, and sometimes, you have a Spirit-led "knowing." However you are sensing God speak to you, go with that.

1. Make yourself comfortable in a chair with as few distractions as possible. Ask God to come and help you as you begin this process. Whatever emotion you are experiencing, give that feeling to God. You can just pray through it or picture yourself handing Him something that symbolizes that emotion to you. If you sense other emotions, then you can give those to Him as well. When you have given Him all of those emotions, then ask Him to fill you

with the opposite: love for anger, courage for fear, hope for despair, etc.

2. If the persistent emotions try to return, then you might be dealing with an entity causing that emotion. In that case, you can pray something along the lines of: "I see you (negative emotion), and I refuse to partner with you or agree with you anymore. I gather up all of this (negative emotion) along with any other entities involved in any way, and I cast the whole package to the cross. I place the blood of Jesus between all of that and me, and I ask you, Father, to fill me with your (opposite of the negative emotion). You can pray this for all of the emotions if you like.

3. Ask God or Jesus to show you the root of this overreaction. He might show you a box, a ball, or a vase—my clients have seen all sorts of containers. You also might have a memory of an event or a sense of what has happened that caused the creation of the part.

4. You want to forgive the person or people who hurt you. You will also need to go through Steps 2 and 3 above for any emotions or entities that are guarding the part and/or are in the part.

5. Ask Jesus to reveal any additional forgiveness or clean-up that you need to do.

6. Fill the part with all of the good things that it has missed out by being hidden away. Ask Jesus to mature the part to the level of the rest of your soul. You want the part to become as clean and whole as possible.

7. You can also hand whatever container you see to Jesus. Sometimes, He takes things away, and sometimes, He re-unites them with the rest of you. You want the part as clean as possible, especially if He reunites the part.

8. Ask for God's grace and nurturing as you learn how to walk in this new area of wholeness.

Chapter 13: Michael

A Few of My Techniques

The Soul-Gem

Often when I integrate various parts, I visualize a large clear or white gemstone, which represents the core self. This stone is chipped and missing large parts of its body. Small chips are floating around it, attached by a golden light or thread. I visualize these chips, representing the fragmented parts, slowly and gently being pulled inward by the golden threads until they fit in the proper spot. Once fitted, I intentionally will them to fuse back into the gem. This desire or intention causes them to practically melt back into place, making them permanently part of the soul-gem without any cracks or lines to show they had ever broken off.

While working with these chips, be sure not to try to connect too many at once; you will likely find they all resist you. When all of them resist together, you will probably not make progress. Try starting with an expectation that the chips that are ready to fuse will be surrounded with a colored light of your choosing. I personally prefer blue as that color represents healing to me. In general, when a chip is ready to fuse, it will more easily be drawn in by the golden thread.

You might find groups of chips clustered together that might even have threads connecting them to each other. You can possibly integrate or fuse the chips with one another, essentially merging fragments together. Not only does this strengthen the fused part, but fewer parts will later need to be reintegrated with the core.

The Initial Fragment Plane

In the past, I began by imagining a large space with a platform in the center on which rested a pillar of gold or blue light with a small version of me in the middle. I view this as my "core self." I envisioned lots of people standing outside the pillar—other versions or aspects of myself that needed to be brought into unity and wholeness. I then mentally willed those fragments to line up and walk up the steps of the platform and into the light. As they walked into the pillar, they were sucked inside my image of my core self. One of the things that surprised me when I did this was just how many fragments were milling around outside the light pillar, hundreds, possibly more. Even when I had them line up and integrate, many more still refused to join.

This process showed me that I was onto something. Typically, when I daydream and imagine something, I am fully in control of what happens because it is all inside my mind. When I engage spiritual reality, not everything responds according to my will simply because other sentient beings are involved whose choices I can't control. In this case, those fragments who chose not to integrate were those who were either not ready or not willing to do so. Sometimes, I tried to force them to integrate anyway, but this was rarely effective as I could sense and even watch them fighting against me.

The Upgraded Fragment Plane

Fast forward years later, I still use a similar integration method, but I have added a few components. First, while I still make use of a "fragment plane"—the open space filled with fragments—I have changed the way I visualize the location. Now, I often imagine myself in the throne room of God with the parts and my core self in front of the Father. Jesus is there, and I ask Him and the angels to help me integrate the fragments, which they do. I begin by asking Jesus to separate all the parts who are ready to integrate at this moment and to have them reintegrate with my core self. Then, I ask the angels to minister to all of the fragments who are close to being ready but who aren't quite there yet. As I give the angels a few minutes, sometimes the parts they are tending to will choose to integrate as well. Finally, I ask Jesus and the angels to work on the ones who aren't ready, especially to reveal Himself to the fragments that don't know Him. I then exit the scene and let them continue working.

Piecing the Puzzle Together

Imagine a large puzzle sitting on a table with a box of pieces nearby and/or laid out on the table. Visualize the border already put in place. This is your core self. Everything else, all the other puzzle pieces, should eventually end up inside the main border. Your job is to work on putting the pieces together.

You might find that you have entire sections of the puzzle already put together whether in the right place inside the border or sitting outside. Find a set of pieces outside the border that are already grouped together. Imagine that section acting as a magnet to draw pieces to its outer edge, making the section even larger.

As with previous methods, consider using colored light as an indicator of which puzzle pieces are ready and to help guide them to the right location. One recommendation is to be intuitive and pay attention to when a puzzle piece is outside and should not be made any larger. It is possible for a part to push down the core self and manifest, so be mindful that the larger the puzzle piece becomes, the more it will be able to exert control on the core. After using the magnet technique, guide the section to its place inside the puzzle borders. You might visualize it being magnetized or glued to the board in the proper location. If the large piece is not ready, visualize immersing it in a cleansing solution, wiping away dirt, or bathing it in a golden or white light. All of these are images that will release healing power into the fragments you are working with to help them integrate into the puzzle.

Emotional Cleansing

Visualize the body with various lights denoting negative emotions. Go through a process of clearing these negatively colored lights out of the body, then filling those spaces back up with positive colors. I prefer to see black and red as harmful colors and golden, blue, or green as life-giving hues. Sometimes the bad colors will not move out easily or might even fight back. This is an indicator of demonic activity, which can either be overpowered, although this is often difficult, or you can work to find the underlying point of access and resolve those negative energies or colors. This should make it easier to clean out that resistant area of color.

All of the methods above will ultimately accomplish the same overall goals, but one image might work better for you than another. I use a number of these methods, depending on my mood or on what strikes me as the most beneficial at that time.

The most recent instance of fragment self-healing occurred for me while I was driving to work. This might seem dangerous to some, but I have become accustomed to engaging the visionary realm while involved in other activities, so I find it relatively safe. What surprised me was that on this particular occasion, as I began to have the fragments integrate, I began to cry. Crying is significant to me because I have found that, when working with fragments, crying indicates effective healing and integration. In the natural, our bodies sometimes release tears when we release negative emotional energies, and the physical composition of these tears differs from when we have something in our eye. Thus, when I found myself crying, this further confirmed to me that this method works and wasn't a figment of my imagination.

The main benefit of self-integration is that I don't have to wait for someone else to walk me through the process. Jesus is the Master-Healer, and if I let Him guide the session, it tends to be effective. Previously, when I didn't understand what I was doing, I tried to force the fragments to integrate via my will, and while it worked for some, others just wouldn't respond, and nothing I did could make them. When Jesus loves them into submission, they willingly go where He leads, and as He is the Good Shepherd, they can trust Him with their safety and well-being when it's time to integrate.

The other important aspect of being Spirit-led in this process and of letting Jesus run the show is that He will often do more than I expect. Most recently, He took three fragments with Him that He indicated needed special attention—far more help than I could provide them on my own. From what I was able to discern, these particular fragments were under heavy demonic bondage. He assured me that, in the right time, He would integrate them with me, but first, He was going to do a deep work in them and set them free.

If fragment self-healing is something you are interested in or have been seeking, consider trying the methods laid out above. If the throne room of God doesn't work for you, try another location. The fragment plane is always an effective option, and you can fill it with healing power and glory light in prayer before you assemble your fragments there. The benefit of the light pillar is that it acts as a protective mechanism for your core self, keeping it inside the pillar. Having the other fragments come to it is an act of submission and/or subservience, which just ensures that no other personalities take over during the integration process. While this doesn't occur often, it can happen, so the protective screen seems to act as a prudent cautionary step.

Chapter 14: Sam

Some Caveats to Working

Alone

While we are hopeful that you will be able to take many of these strategies and implement them in your process of healing, we don't believe that all inner healing can or should be completed on your own. There are several reasons for this.

First, you will often experience internal resistance toward making any positive changes, especially when dealing with deep wounds. Remember that these fragments are stuck in time and still believe that the trauma is occurring or will be occurring again soon. The fragments might not allow you to access the content that you need to in order to heal.

Second, if we've been under the influence of a lie for a long time, especially when it comes to generational issues, then we might not be able to see the lie for what it is and therefore won't be able to grasp the truth and apply it to our lives. We need someone from the outside with a different perspective to help us to recognize and conquer the lies we are believing.

Third, if the woundings are particularly traumatic or difficult for you to face, and you can't get to that area, you might need a helping hand to keep you focused on moving through the trauma to the healing on the other side. If you feel as though you are getting stuck, then please stop and seek assistance. Healing from trauma should not re-traumatize you. It might be difficult and be a process, but if you struggle with a lack of hope, then you need to find someone's hope to borrow.

We invite you to listen to all of us in this book and work through as much as you can on your own.

Section 3:

Where the Rubber
Meets the Road

Chapter 15: Matt

Healing From Tragedy

Previously, Jason had several prayer sessions with me when some of his fractured parts were healed and integrated. He wanted further ministry because he was still struggling with irrational fears that were destroying his relationships.

What I was seeing in the spirit around him was an over-protective bubble, a shield he used to keep people out. He confirmed that he did maintain a lot of distance from folks due to his fear of being hurt. I walked him through emotionally tracing that fear back to the first time in his life when he felt exactly that way. By turning "off" his logical mind as much as possible, just feeling his emotions, and paying attention to where this fear spontaneously originated, he ended up at a memory of his first job.

Jason was ten years old when he began working at a rodeo, trying to perform semi-adult responsibilities. In this memory, he was yelled at and judged harshly by his superiors who expected a lot from such a young boy. We eliminated the shame, fear, and rejection from this memory by simply trusting the Lord to remove it. Once the negative emotions were removed, we invited the Lord to come into the memory to minister to Jason.

Jason had a picture in his mind of Jesus showing up and comforting him with a message that He had always been present with him. This message was very relevant because he had felt alone and subject to judgment ever since. He had suffered many physical injuries in his early life as well, including severe internal injuries after being trampled by a cow, and he had blamed God for these. Jesus showed Jason how He was with him even when he had been trampled. He shared that He was the one helping Jason's dad jump down from a platform to rescue him.

I asked Jason to come out of agreement with the lie that God was behind his suffering, the lie that God was to blame for it. Jason wanted to follow through, but he became aware of some serious resistance coming from within him. This turned out to be a fractured part behind this resistance, a part who was very angry at the Lord for all the tragedies and suffering he had endured.

We began doing simple memory healing but ran into an area where a fractured part was carrying the painful emotions. At times, such memory healing doesn't seem to be working no matter what we try, and in many cases, this is because a fractured part is carrying the issues and refusing to let them go. In these cases, you must work with the part to help them become willing to receive healing.

I called out to the fractured part, who began to share with me how angry he was about all the injuries as well as about various problems he had in school. Though he was angry at the Father, he was surprisingly okay with meeting Jesus. As Jesus revealed himself to the part and the part began to ask Jesus about the suffering he had endured, Jesus shared that it was the enemy who caused all the accidents and suffering, not God.

The part responded, "Then why did you allow that to happen?"

Jesus replied, "I didn't. I gave man authority over these things, but the people in your life didn't understand how to pray to stop them. They were caught up in dead religion and weren't open to the truth. They were just locked in bondage to what they'd been taught." The part was weeping, and Jesus was weeping with him.

Now, the fractured part gave Jesus permission to remove the anger he held toward God, which was quickly removed. The part had binoculars, and he wanted me to look through them and tell him what I saw. I looked through them by faith and told him that I saw a mountain on an island. He referred to this mountain as "Fiji." When I had him ask Jesus what that meant, he replied that it was about isolation and about getting away from people to avoid hurt.

The part gave Jesus permission to take away all the hurts. The island was suddenly uprooted and placed among people. Although it was still a tropical paradise, at the same time, the part was now in a place where it could reach people, be productive, and fulfill destiny. Jason now had a sense of this part of him being on "island time," which, to him, meant being in a state of internal rest while still being able to accomplish what he needed to do among people.

After all this, Jason reported finding release from the fears with which he had been struggling.

Chapter 16: Sam

Two-For-One Healing

As I worked more in the Spirit and visually in various types of healing situations, I began to find that I was led to move similarly for the healing of fragments as well. During one of those experiences, I came to my prayer time with concerns for myself as well as a friend. Once Jesus shows up, you never know what direction events will go. In this case, I was led to minister healing to not only myself, but also on behalf of that friend. The story follows:

I close my eyes and am walking in the spirit along the path in the woods again. I come across a large bowl on a stone pedestal. Angels come and fill a pitcher with water from a spring nearby, carrying it to fill a basin made of alabaster or a similar material. Another angel has towels, so I come to the bowl and wash. As I dry off, another angel hands me a white robe and new sandals. I put them on, and the angels take away the first basin. I assume they are cleaning it. Two other angels come with another basin, but this one is crystal, lovely, and transparent. The angels coming after them have two large golden pitchers filled with something that sparkles and glows. They stand at opposite sides and pour in this liquid. One stream is red, and the other is blue. They swirl together down into the bowl and turn purple briefly, then fade to clear, all the while as the liquid glows and sparkles. The angels nod to me and then leave, and I am there all alone.

I feel a breeze in the trees, and I know the Spirit is coming. He comes and stirs the water, which flashes with all sorts of colors, like a liquid diamond. He smiles and winks at me. Jesus and the Father arrive, and all four of us are standing around the basin, which is about 4 feet tall, so I can see into it easily although I can't lean over it.

The Father reaches over and puts his hand on my shoulder. Jesus does the same. I feel the apprehension about what's going to happen leave me. "Are you ready?" I nod although I'm not entirely sure. They laugh, which makes me laugh, and then I am ready.

I look into the basin, and I can see a small girl in the corner of a cave. She is sitting among the shards of what might be glass bottles and pottery vases. I watch myself go to her and give her a hug. As I do so, she is absorbed into me. Jesus hands me a broom and dust bin, and I sweep up the shards of broken dreams and promises. I dump them in a bin and then hand them to Jesus a bit reluctantly. I look at Him apologetically, and He smiles kindly. He takes the bin and holds it briefly but then sets it down and reaches inside. I'm a bit worried that He will cut Himself, but He pulls out what looks like a shield.

The design is a mosaic that expands as it comes out of the bin. I can see all the pieces that were in the bin now arranged in a beautiful design. When it is all before me, I can see that the shield is big enough to cover all of me. Jesus then pulls out a matching crown. I wonder wondering how I'm going to carry them since they look so heavy. Then, I hear the Father laugh and feel the breeze of the Spirit again. I look up to find the cave has gone. Jesus places the crown on my head and adjusts the shield on my front, and He then puts a similar one on my back. As He does so, I can see them connect like armor, becoming very thin and light, almost invisible.

The Spirit then leads us back to the basin. I look in it again and see the client that I met with yesterday, Bea. She is surrounded by younger versions of herself. They see us coming and some run and hide behind her. Others stand in front of her as if to protect her. I see some demons in her midsection although they are trying to hide. I'm not able to reach them because of the small ones in front.

Jesus brings out large pads of paper and crayons. He starts to color, and I do so as well. We start to sing, and some of the Guardians start to smile and sing as well. I tell them that they can come and color; there is plenty of room. I reassure them that Bea will be fine because angels are all around. Slowly, a couple of them at a time join us and start to color. A few angels bring easels, canvas, and paint, and a few more angels come and start to paint. The angels start to sing along, and more of them begin to dance around the easels and the coloring on the ground. The scene is and feels a bit chaotic.

I look over at Bea and notice that only one girl is standing with her now. She's about fifteen and is holding her stomach. I can see that a large demon has a knife in her and is maliciously twisting it. I ask her if she wants it to leave, and she nods. I gesture to a couple of angels who grab the demon and fling him far away. They reach inside of her and pull out several smaller demons as well, chaining them all together and grab them as they head in the direction they threw the other one. I assume they are going to gather him up as they leave.

Two other angels come and anoint her with oil, cleaning all of the wounds that are now visible. As they do so, she begins to laugh. Then, she joins hands with them, and they dance off. I stand beside Bea, and we watch all the little ones play. I ask her if she wants to be well, and she answers affirmatively but admits that she's afraid. I smile and laugh, "Don't be afraid," I tell her. "It will be different but very, very good."

She has been holding her stomach and then pulls out critters. She hands the critters to the angels who are present. I grab some as well, and the angels bind them up, and when they are all out, they take the critters away. Jesus comes and touches all of her wounds. I can see His blood flowing from His hands into all of her wounds, healing them and infusing His DNA into them. I speak peace to her, and she breathes a deep sigh.

The three of us turn and look at the creative chaos in front of us. All the little girls are laughing and dancing and creating. Jesus tells Bea that she can leave them here if she likes; He'll look after them. She smiles and nods and fades away.

Jesus looks at me, and we smile and join in the dance. Soon, all the girls are dancing, and I stop to watch once again. He smiles and winks at me, and dances off into the trees with all of them following behind, just like the Pied Piper. I see a few of mine run after them, and then, I close my eyes and am back.

Chapter 17: Matt

My Explanation of Guardians
and Protectors

One day, while mowing the lawn in my early teens, I was given a glimpse of three major identities within me. This was a very clear awareness that spontaneously came to the surface of my mind.

I began to see one identity who performed, trying to be super cool. Another identity carried the hurts that I didn't even want to acknowledge, and yet another identity within me was like a Guardian or a Protector. I sensed a lot of insight into who I was behind this sudden revelation, yet I had no grid for such things at that young age. Could I really have three identities within me? Who had ever heard of such a thing? This was just my imagination conjuring up these strange images and ideas, right?

As an adult, I was led into the healing of many more than just three fragments/fractured parts. I thought that maybe those three I glimpsed earlier were just a few of those parts. Why did I only see three? Why did I have a sense that these three made up who I was as a whole?

Only in recent years, when I attended a training seminar by Andrew Miller of HeartSync Ministries, did I begin to understand the meaning of that early revelation. As I prayed into this issue further, first by myself and then with various other people, I've received multiple clear confirmations that we really do have three separate identities, not just one. When Scripture records that we were made in the image of God, it wasn't kidding. God is a Trinity, three persons in one. Apparently, we are also a trinity in this sense.

Dr. Tom Hawkins, a pioneer in working with ritual abuse survivors, first discovered that they had three identities at the core of their being, identities different in nature than the rest of their fractured parts. Diane sat under his teaching while he was still alive and heard this from him.

Andrew Miller, who has also worked with many RA survivors since 1990, gained experience in healing these "core" identities. He discovered that they weren't just present in RA survivors but in the general population as well. His terms for these "primary" core identities are Function, Emotion, and Guardian.

Function is the identity who handles daily tasks, complex skills, and left-brain/intellectual activities in general. Emotion is the identity who carries our emotional trauma and connects empathetically, handling more right-brain activities. Guardian is the identity who guards our hearts, discerns safety or danger, and decides who feels trustworthy enough to open up to. Guardian is also associated with the fight-or-flight response in the lower, "primitive" part of the brain.

Some people I've prayed with have explained this as follows:

- The Function Identity associates with the mind
- The Guardian Identity associates with the will
- The Emotion Identity associates with the emotions.

At the same time, Function, Emotion, and Guardian each have their own aspects of mind, will, and emotions, so this subject isn't as simplistic as some would like to make it. HeartSync is a great ministry to learn much more on the subject of these core identities and how to heal them although their approach differs significantly from mine.

Guardian/Protector parts are often angry at God for the hard things that have happened in a person's life, especially those tragedies responsible for their original woundedness and fracturing. At first, they might refuse to receive help from Jesus due to this anger yet, many times, will welcome an opportunity to confront Jesus in person and to demand answers for why He "allowed" a disaster to happen in their life. Take this opportunity to invite Him to reveal Himself to them, to let Him give them helpful answers, and to melt down their defenses with His love.

Jesus' answer is often different, tailored to each person and each fractured part, but I've regularly seen Him share some version of, "That wasn't from me," or "I didn't allow that; people did it of their own free choice." The conversation might be more detailed as the part has more questions and as Jesus answers, but He is typically able to get through to them quickly in this way.

I had one client who had suffered tremendously due to disabling physical conditions from birth. His Christian parents had always taught him that God had a special purpose for his great suffering as part of a divinely ordained higher plan. Besides this horrible teaching, he carried tremendous shame and always felt as if God were punishing him for something he did wrong. This client had been taught a very hurtful theology in church and even in Bible college—God afflicts His people with diseases and birth defects, especially when He's mad at them.

Even when Jesus told this man's fractured parts that they had been taught wrongly, that God never does any of those things, they still demanded more evidence. They demanded to be shown the record of their purpose in heaven to see if birth defects and diseases were found in the books written about their destiny. Jesus obliged and showed them the record of the Father's purpose and destiny for them. Birth defects weren't found anywhere in the writings nor was any mention of suffering or any kind of disease. Only joyful plans and experiences were written in God's purpose for this man's early life.

Before the client's parts became bold enough to demand that Jesus show them the records in heaven, they needed to take some "baby steps." I encouraged them to be upfront with Jesus. I even suggested that they follow through with their idea of putting Jesus on trial, demanding answers for why so many hard things had happened to them.

When Jesus let them put Him on trial, answering all their tough, accusing questions from a witness stand with His absolute gentleness and perfect wisdom, they became much more receptive to His help as well as more comfortable sharing exactly how they felt with Him.

This man's journey was a little more outside the box than I'm used to, with all sorts of regular, in-depth interactions with angels and other unusual heavenly experiences. At one point, his parts even took it upon themselves to interview various angels and beings from heaven, asking if any of them had ever seen Jesus or the Father put sickness upon anyone. None of the angels or heavenly witnesses could testify of Jesus or the Father ever causing sickness or birth defects.

After all the bold tests, this man's angry parts became willing to cooperate with the Lord, to let him remove their anger and to receive healing. His life has drastically changed for the better as he has allowed the Lord to begin healing him from the inside out in these deeper areas.

I haven't yet found anyone else who needed that much convincing. Often, even the very sight of Jesus and His relational style is enough to persuade fractured parts that He is trustworthy, that He is the answer rather than the problem. You might be able to answer objections yourself, but if you do, always use this to lead the parts into a direct encounter with the Lord. He is the one who will meet their deepest needs and restore their trust most effectively.

Parts might also be in a very fearful state, afraid to even let Jesus reveal Himself to them. They might believe a religious message that God is scary and condemning. They might carry shame and be afraid of letting Jesus see them as they are. The Lord isn't going to violate their will or impose Himself upon them when they don't want Him to.

Many times, I need to share some good news in these cases—Jesus isn't mean or condemning; He won't force them to do anything they aren't ready for; He will only love them and make them feel better. Sometimes, I've had to ask their permission to let Jesus reveal Himself from a distance, a little bit at a time, and then to give the parts time to invite Him closer as they became ready.

With Guardian/Protector parts, you might need to share with them that Jesus won't take away their role of protecting the person, but He will empower them to do so more effectively. He created each person with a Guardian aspect of them for a reason.

You might also need to ask for the parts' permission so that you can remove fear and shame or even remove demonic entities causing fear and shame within them through a command of faith. Once the overwhelming emotions are calmed down, you will likely have more success with inviting Jesus to reveal Himself and to minister to the parts since they will be more willing to let Him do that.

I've found that healing a person's Guardian Identity is tremendously powerful in getting past their defense mechanisms, including denial, anxiety, anger, blame-shifting, distraction, overwhelm, etc., which are often preventing them from receiving healing of their deep wounds.

The Story of James' Guardian Set Free

James was molested by a group of older relatives at a very young age, so young that he had no concept of how to process it at the time. He didn't know what to say to his parents amid his overwhelming emotions, so he said nothing. However, he began showing signs of extreme duress: acting out and being unwilling to get up and go to school in the mornings. He was taken to see a Christian psychologist.

Session after session, he was unable to express anything to his counselor, and he didn't see much hope for healing. When he realized how much these sessions were costing his poor parents, he made a decision not to burden them. He stuffed his hurts deep inside, pretended to feel okay and just willed himself to get up each morning and go through life, despite all the pain he was carrying. This decision stuck with him until I prayed with him as an adult.

James was receiving healing and finding spiritual breakthroughs, yet our sessions were often difficult. When we started to get to the root of an issue, he became distracted, suddenly feeling a need to spend ten to twenty minutes rambling about something totally unrelated. He grew angry, had theological arguments, became overwhelmingly tired, or looked for any reason to avoid dealing with the issues.

Still, we made progress, and we were seeing major, legitimate breakthroughs in his life. Once, I was even able to talk to a fractured "Protector" part of him who was responsible for some of this resistance and to walk that part through resolving a past issue. James told me that he was on cloud nine with all the freedom, healing, and personal achievements resulting from these sessions.

He then attended a few family functions and ran into the relatives who had molested him, whom he hadn't seen for decades. He felt fine with it at the time but, several days later, became deeply tormented. All of his old, overwhelming emotions from that young age came to the surface. He began hearing accusing voices telling him to kill himself. He began struggling mentally and emotionally, taking up a substance addiction as a means of escape.

He desperately wanted freedom from this debilitating pain and torment. However, as we began praying, his mind wandered everywhere else instead of focusing on what we were doing. This was despite his tearful statements about how much he needed freedom in his life. I thought this distraction was likely his Guardian at work and that his Guardian was probably under demonic influence, being manipulated and even controlled to stop the healing of his issues and strongholds.

I explained the concept of the Guardian Identity to James. I then began talking out loud to his Guardian, sharing that I understood how he was only trying to protect James in the best ways he knew how. I shared that I wasn't there to try and take away his job of protecting but to help him do it more effectively. Guardians often need to understand this key issue before they are willing to cooperate. They are often afraid of losing their job, leaving the person unprotected.

I prayed and commanded all demonic influence to be bound and held back from the Guardian so that he could make his own decision to cooperate or not. Instantly, the distractions stopped, remaining a non-issue throughout the rest of our prayer time.

I shared with him (Guardian) that he must have been working so hard for a very important reason, that he must have had something very important to protect in James' heart. I asked him to share his concerns with me.

In response to my request, James suddenly saw how his Guardian learned to act the way it did. He shared the information about his childhood that I had mentioned earlier, how he had been taken to counseling with no results, and how he had then made the decision to suppress his emotions, pretending to be okay so that he wouldn't burden his parents. His Guardian, the part of him in charge of keeping the feelings suppressed, had helped James to survive many years using these tactics to deny access to his deepest wounds.

I shared with James' Guardian that those methods were effective when he was a little kid—when he didn't have the maturity to deal with serious issues and didn't know how to invite the Lord to heal those areas. He didn't have anyone to walk him through that, but his present situation was totally different. I shared that he had been manipulated by the enemy to prevent the Lord from healing him.

I asked Guardian how his relationship was with Jesus, and he responded to James' mind that he had no relationship even though James had been a believer for most of his life. I told him that he had been standing against demonic attacks all this time, engaging in spiritual warfare with only his human strength, and getting beaten up as a result. I shared with him that there was a better way. He could be empowered by Jesus to have authority over the enemy, making him much more effective as a Guardian.

He jumped on this offer to have a relationship with the Lord and to be empowered by him to overcome the enemy. As James prayed, inviting the Lord to come into the heart of the Guardian aspect of him, trusting him to be Lord and Savior of this part of his heart, he felt a sensation he recognized as God's presence washing through him and doing something significant.

I led James' Guardian to give Jesus permission to heal him, to remove all demonic presences, and to remove all traumas and negative issues, and then we prayed, trusting the Lord to do just that. I was also sure to extend the offer to any other parts of James, any other facets of his heart or fractured parts of himself who were willing to receive the same kind of healing his Guardian had just received. We prayed once again for the Lord to do all these things for any parts of James who were willing to receive. We prayed a few more things, inviting Holy Spirit to move, to cleanse, to heal, to free James overall, and I was led to break several specific generational strongholds.

James immediately reported feeling much greater freedom and more at ease than he had felt in a long time. I soon received a call from him, testifying that the spiritual attacks, the overwhelming negative emotions, and the suicidal thoughts had all left his life completely after that one prayer session. He felt that his life had instantly gone from night to day. He shared that even his reacquired substance addiction had suddenly vanished.

This is an example of the powerful outcomes that can occur when you reach someone's Guardian aspect of self, which results in the dropping of unhealthy defenses, learning to trust, and allowing the Lord access to heal deeper hurts. Working with the Guardian as well as with fractured "Protector" parts who play similar roles to the Guardian has become a typical element of my inner healing ministry. I and others have found this an effective way to bring down seemingly impenetrable walls.

Chapter 18: Matt

Lessons From Jenn's Process

A friend and I were praying for a young woman's healing. "Jenn" had wanted to be healed from one painful condition that had stumped her doctors: an inflamed, ulcerated bladder. She seemed destined to suffer with it long term.

It was a great day. As we prayed for her using simple, Spirit-led commands of faith, she was not only instantly healed of all symptoms of the ulcerated bladder long term but from an additional seven or eight other physical conditions as well. We noticed that not only was all the pain related to the ulcerated bladder gone, but the visible bloating had subsided, and the appearance of her lower abdomen had returned to normal.

She also had a frozen shoulder and was unable to lift her arm past the armpit level. Her shoulder was quickly healed through prayer so that she could raise her arm overhead without pain.

As we resolved several other physical problems, we were led to address various emotional issues. We did this by tracing emotions back to their source in earlier memories and then handing over the pain and anger found in them to the Lord so that He could remove it based on the work of the cross. Standing on the scriptural promises that Jesus is "the Lamb of God who takes away the sin of the world" (John 1:29) and that He "has borne our griefs and carried our sorrows" (Isaiah 53:4 NKJV), we were quickly and simply removing one deep emotional problem after another. (Details on how to walk through this process are shared in the upcoming pages.) After eliminating emotional wounds in this way, we continued going after more outward issues, seeing more physical healing.

We were also led to pray for Jenn's digestive system, and I had an image of the Lord giving her a bowl of cereal to eat. She replied that a bowl of cereal was one of her favorite foods to eat, but she had terrible problems in her gut if she dared to eat cereal. Since her faith had been encouraged by all the other miracles she had just experienced, she agreed to eat a bowl of cereal soon. When I heard back from her a week later, she said that she had been eating cereal without any problem whatsoever.

At the end of the day, she received many internal and external breakthroughs, but we still couldn't resolve one neurological problem. She was unable to flex one of her feet and her toes in a certain way, and this condition didn't respond much to any type of prayer we tried. She walked around limping everywhere she went due to this stubborn issue.

On to the Fractured Parts

I was invited back to pray with Jenn another day, and before meeting with her, I asked the Lord what He wanted to deal with. I had a sense that part of her was fractured with a young teenage girl on the inside of her. When we met up, I discerned something different. I wasn't picking up on a teenage girl anymore but on a baby who needed to be warmed up in some way. I began questioning whether I was just off since what I was sensing wasn't consistent.

I asked her to become quiet and see what responded as I tried to call a child inside her to the surface. I asked her to pay attention to any thoughts, feelings, or images coming to the surface as I called out to any fractured part within her. Her part in this, as described, looked just like listening to the Lord but was focused on listening to a part of her. For the first time, she became aware of a teenage girl inside her with some strong emotions.

I tried to talk to the teenage girl and invite Jesus to reveal Himself to her, but Jenn shared with me that a dark presence was blocking the girl from communicating with me. This demon got in the way and spoke to the mind of the woman being ministered to, swearing at me, and threatening me from within her.

Defaulting to previous knowledge and experience, I began sharing that Jesus wanted to cut the ties between this evil being and her, freeing her from it if she would only give Him permission.

This is typical of situations with fractured parts. The demonic tricks them into making agreements of some kind, possibly disguising themselves as another fractured part or even as Jesus Himself to trick the parts. The fractured part need only renounce any agreements with the demon/s and give Jesus permission to remove them, and He does.

This time, Jenn relayed back to me that this part of her was trying to give Jesus permission, but the demon was still not leaving. This wasn't typical. I needed to find out what the real issue was.

I asked the teenager to ask Jesus what He was saying that she needed to do to get rid of this thing. She reported back to me through the adult woman that she heard Him say, "Give your heart."

Apparently, this teenage part had not yet given her heart to the Lord. This can also be a common issue with fractured parts. They might not have given their heart to Jesus. They might not be born again even though the main personality of the "host" has. As soon as the teenage part gave her heart to Jesus, the demon was removed, and I was then able to talk with her without interference.

Jenn expressed being especially grateful for this. She was quite spiritually sensitive, so she had known for a while that she had a "darkness" inside her, and now she was aware that it was finally gone.

A Teaching Moment: Teenagers and Their Pets

Among fractured parts, teenagers are often found to be "Protectors," which means that they have become responsible for keeping other, more vulnerable parts of the person safe. They do exactly what the "Guardian" Core Identity does except as a fractured part rather than as an aspect of the core. Some people call these "hidden Guardians."

You will most likely run into some variety of "Protector" early on as you are beginning to talk with somebody's parts or when you are becoming close to a very vulnerable area. These types of fractured parts might take on the form of warriors with swords or other weapons; tough guys; scary animals, such as bears or dogs; monsters, such as ogres; or teenagers. A person may form Guardians/Protectors in any image their mind chooses. One man I prayed with even seemed to have a Protector who took on the form of a Stormtrooper from Star Wars!

I don't think that most teenage Protector parts result from woundedness during the person's teenage years, though I might be wrong, but I think the teenagers are often formed because they are typically given a bit more leeway when it comes to bad attitudes, anger, rudeness, and rebellion. A teenage persona might be seen as more effective at putting up relational walls and keeping others away from vulnerable places. This is usually the role they perform for the person. Of course, the demonic loves to join in and "help" them with this task.

Freeing a Guardian/Protector part from the demonic is often the first necessary step in working with them. It sure makes the process a lot easier. They are regularly manipulated and even controlled by demons and won't be able to cooperate much until they receive some freedom. These days, before even talking with a Protector, I will typically use a quick prayer to bind and restrain the demonic from manipulating or controlling the parts. I will then ask permission from the Guardian/Protector part to send all the demons away for good and cast them out with a simple command to "go."

Notice that my first step is not to command the demons to leave or to just rebuke the demon in the Name of Jesus. Instead, I specifically pray to restrain the demonic from manipulating or controlling the Protector parts. At this point, I or the person receiving prayer will often notice a change in the fractured Protector part, recognizing that it softens up or even completely changes into another form.

Since the demonic can no longer control the Protectors, they are now free to make their own decisions and almost always want the demons gone. Guardians/Protectors hate being controlled by anyone, especially demons, and you just need to ask their permission so that you can order the critters to leave.

After evicting the demonic, the parts will often soften up or change further. Many times, the image of a hardened warrior or monster will disappear, and a hurting child will be left in its place, asking for healing.

The will of the fractured parts is of utmost importance in determining whether you can free them from the demonic in this way or not. In fact, a person's or part's agreement in some way is the only reason that the enemy has the power to operate in their lives at all. If you know your authority in Christ and once the person or their part comes out of agreement with the enemy, he immediately loses all ability to resist a command to go.

As in Jenn's story so far, the fractured part might need to receive Jesus as Savior or to verbally break agreements made with the enemy. In rarer cases, the person and/or their part might need to agree to generationally renounce specific pacts made with the enemy by their ancestors. Usually, it isn't that complicated.

Demons are often strapped to the parts' backs, pretending to be their friends, and the parts might need to break agreements with them and give permission for them to be removed at some point. These don't seem to cause anywhere near as much trouble as the ones I work on removing at the beginning, but they will still put up some resistance. The parts might not even know that these are demons at first, so they might need an explanation or have this otherwise revealed to them in some way. One clue to the real identity of any impostors is that they tend to be mean to the parts.

Parts in Relationship with the Demonic

If parts are unwilling to break agreement with demons or with whatever the demons are disguised as, I've found it effective to use a declaration of authority in Christ to expose their true nature. You can expose a demon disguised as something else for what it really is. If the parts know that the demons are demons yet have grown attached to having them around, you can even use a command of authority to expose the true intentions of the demons toward the parts. I've found some parts who wanted to keep their critters before their true intentions were revealed, but they changed their minds when they found out the demons' true agendas.

124

At times, the demons were meeting a need the parts had, such as companionship, entertainment, a promise of safety, etc., and the Lord had to show up and offer them a better way of meeting those needs before the parts let Him remove them. I've also found that helping free the parts from some of their issues even while the demons are restrained but still present can bring them to a place of greater cooperation in order to remove the evil spirits.

If the demonic influence is so heavy that parts can't speak to you, you can have them just raise a hand, wiggle a finger, or even just say "yes" in their hearts to give the Lord permission to remove them. Some of the critters won't go until a part resolves a specific issue, such as anger, fear, or self-hatred, but most seem to leave on command if you only receive a part's permission.

By evicting the demonic early on, you can free up the part to begin receiving healing from the Lord without the hindrance and interference that they would experience otherwise. Ministry tends to go a lot more smoothly after that.

I also try to introduce parts to Jesus as soon as possible, as in Jenn's case. He or another member of the Trinity can appear to them in any form they need. Some aren't comfortable with a man or with a Christian religious figure and need to meet Him in a more nontraditional form.

I ask the part's permission for Jesus to reveal Himself to them and to begin ministering to them, and then I pray in faith that He will immediately do it. The person might have an image in their imagination of the Lord coming and ministering to their parts, or the parts themselves might see Jesus while the core personality cannot. Either way, the parts can share how the interaction is going by communicating thoughts, feelings, and/or images expressed to the person's mind. The Lord really does meet with the parts and begin walking them through healing in these cases.

Sometimes, as with Jenn, everything flows smoothly and easily. Jesus is immediately present; everybody knows it, and the part begins receiving help and answers from Him. Other times, you might need to work through obstacles before a part will be receptive to a conversation with the Lord.

Back to Jenn's Story

I began asking the Lord to reveal what He wanted to do for this teenager within Jenn to heal her further. Before she would be ready to be integrated into the adult personality, she needed to be fully healed. I asked her to pose this question to Jesus and to report back what He said.

When working with fractured parts, I am always looking for Jesus to bring thorough, complete healing and cleansing to the parts before integrating them. This way, the woundedness that caused them to fracture, as well as any other problem issues picked up throughout their life, will not be integrated into the core person. Only the healthy aspects that were previously separated will be integrated.

Jesus can quickly take away any hurts or issues if the fractured part is only willing to hand them over to Him. He simply takes them away, and they have no more presence or effect. I tell people, tongue in cheek, to "think of it like Jesus is magical." He heals parts faster and more easily than any therapy known on earth. We just need to have enough of a grid for that to invite Him to heal. He doesn't temporarily block the issues from our awareness, but He removes them forever.

Often, many issues need to be handed over to Him, which might take the majority of your time in a prayer session for the Lord to identify each one and answer any objections the parts may have to handing them over. Even though it might be tempting to integrate the parts right away and move on to the next parts after a few big problems are resolved, being thorough and sure to heal all their issues will produce the best results by far for the person to whom you are ministering.

The process can become more complicated when the parts are deceived and unwilling to cooperate with Jesus. He might need to take some time to reveal who He truly is and to address various lies they believe about Him. I try to rely on Him revealing truth directly to the part. You can typically ask their permission to find out what He has to say about a subject and then invite Him to speak to them rather than trying to counsel the fractured parts on your own.

I don't look for Jesus to heal the parts by uncovering all the lies they believe behind their woundedness and explain truth in all those areas. I don't look to explore memories and invite Jesus into them. None of that is necessary; it would take too long and could be extremely painful and even significantly traumatic for some people. I look for Jesus to address only the deceptions or concerns preventing the parts from being willing to cooperate with Him and then to lead them in handing over all their hurts and issues to Him for removal.

Once the parts trust Jesus, they can begin receiving rapid healing of all their hurts and issues. In Jenn's case, if I remember correctly, her teenage part only held one or two emotional issues, which were quickly removed. I think she was only concerned about the care of another younger fractured part, and she needed to hand the worry and responsibility of that to the Lord.

Jenn told me that she had just become aware that the teenager inside her was carrying a baby in her arms. The teenager was a caretaker for this baby. She became aware that this baby was another fractured part of her, coming from a time when she was left alone in a freezing attic for several days as an infant.

Now I understood why I had perceived a teenager inside Jenn before coming over to pray, and when I arrived, I perceived an infant who needed warming up. I had not shared this with Jenn before she saw it herself. The teen girl was led to hand over the baby girl to Jesus, who warmed her up and brought healing to her as He held her.

Babies are commonly found among fractured parts and might contain heavy woundedness that is foundational to a person's issues. One of the challenges when ministering to the baby parts is that they must choose to receive your help or the Lord's help, but they are too young to understand spoken language. In order to receive their permission to be healed and delivered, someone must communicate with them nonverbally.

The good news is that various options can all potentially work. The core person or one of their parts might soothe the baby and hand it over to the Lord as in Jenn's case. The Lord might be invited to meet with the baby directly, or an angel might be sent to the baby, or you might send a message in the spirit to the baby yourself.

Many times, parts of a person will experience conflicts, and the baby might resist help from the adult from which they were originally fractured, perceiving them as a threat. In some cases, due to fear or demonic agreements, the baby won't let the Lord near, either. The Lord respects the baby's will to choose and will not force His way into the situation. These most obvious options might not always work.

I often make a declaration of faith that I am sending a certain message to the baby, asking its permission to evict all the bad guys and bring healing. After removing the junk, they will likely be much more receptive to the Lord. As in Jenn's case, I usually seek the baby's permission to be handed over to the Lord so that He can complete its healing at some point even if I am already making progress.

Now that both of these parts were completely freed and healed up, Jesus was saying that they were ready to be integrated into the core woman from whom they originally came.

In these situations, I am careful to ask Jesus and to have the parts ask Jesus if they are truly ready to be integrated or if there are any remaining issues that need healing. I don't want to integrate woundedness into the person receiving ministry, which can happen. I want to heal the parts from their woundedness first so that integration will be a positive step for them.

More recently, I've learned to use an open-ended question at this point rather than a closed "yes or no" question. This reduces the opportunity for people to convey "yes" when Jesus is saying "no." If I have the person's part listen for Jesus' answer to, "Is so and so ready to be integrated, or is there something else you want to do for them first?" people seem to hear more accurately. Since we are dealing with human beings, they can easily manufacture their own answers to "yes or no" questions.

Fractured parts might also be afraid of integration. They might think it will mean they will die. They are actually going to be brought more to life. Instead of being stuffed away and only coming to the surface when they are triggered or called upon to perform their function, they will be "out" all the time as part of the whole person, living as one. The part might need a clear explanation of this.

I am careful to ask the parts themselves if they have any questions, unsettled emotions, pain, or areas where Jesus needs to minister before integration. If you leave these areas unresolved, the parts might play along and pretend to be transitioning into integration, but they are only going into hiding because they aren't comfortable yet.

With fractured parts, you might be dealing with young and immature, very wounded and fearful parts of a person. It might take time to earn their trust and to walk them through taking all their issues to the Lord as they become comfortable doing so.

Sometimes, if a fractured part is still fearful and still carries significant trust issues, they might even intentionally lie to you, saying that Jesus told them they are ready to be integrated. It isn't the end of the world if they integrate too early, but the person will still have whatever issues the part was hiding from you and will need to resolve those issues on their own rather than receiving healing separately for the fractured part.

As I'm leading parts through interaction with Jesus, I will often ask the Lord to show me what issues remain, and if they say they are ready to be integrated while these issues are still unresolved, I will know that something is off. They tend to admit the truth if I ask them, "Do you still have (insert spiritually perceived issue)?"

Also, instead of just telling the part to be integrated, I will typically ask Jesus to lead the part into integration, which gives Him an opportunity to lead them somewhere else first or to indicate a need to wait as I've found Him doing at times when parts wrongly thought they were ready.

As soon as the teenager and the baby were integrated into Jenn, her stubborn neurological problem was immediately healed. She began walking in circles around her home, excited that she was finally able to walk without a limp, her previously stuck foot now functioning fully like the other one.

Although a friend and I had previously seen success with many other of this woman's healing needs, her fractured parts needed to be healed and integrated for this particular healing to take place. As far as I know, her healing, internal and external in these areas, remained stable for the long term.

This is an example of a very easy integration. This all can become much more complicated and difficult, depending on where the person is at spiritually, how many and what kind of issues their parts have, etc.

"Life," as They Call It, Happened, then Life Happened

I didn't pray with Jenn again for more than six months. During that time, she became involved in a relationship with an emotionally abusive man, and some of her old physical symptoms began to reoccur. During the emotional attacks in this relationship, her shoulder and neck became painful and frozen once again, although the other healings she experienced during our prayer time remained intact.

She was planning to go through expensive and temporarily debilitating surgery on her shoulder, the same shoulder that I had prayed over before and seen her raise above her head. She was also now seeing a Christian counselor who had diagnosed her with PTSD due to earlier abusive relationships. She described being in constant "hyper-alert" mode, always on the lookout for danger.

Praying with her again, we traced the emotions of her hyper-alert mode, as well as those related to previous abusive relationships, back to their sources in earlier memories. The traumas, fears, and anger in her life she was experiencing, as well as those she was dealing with in memories of her abusive adult relationships, were only emotional echoes of childhood memories. These memories were related to an abusive stepdad along with other situations.

I took about fifteen to twenty minutes to listen to her, walk her through tracing those emotions back to their roots in her original childhood traumas, and to trust the Lord to take away the painful emotions. She also found relief from her PTSD symptoms, including the hyper-alert mode and her negative emotions due to abusive relationships. As these emotional issues were healed, her neck and shoulder suddenly relaxed again and stopped hurting her.

Apparently, her earlier healing in these areas had only been in the physical, but underlying emotional roots still caused tension, leading to the later return of the symptoms when she faced similar stress.

When we finally dealt with these emotional issues, she maintained healing for the long term. This situation is common.

When this occurs, we can at first be tempted to think that the original healing wasn't real, that it was a mental trick or a false sign. However, we just need to keep pressing in and resolve the source of the problem rather than only the symptoms. The recurrence didn't mean that God hadn't resolved her symptoms in the first place or that He was teasing her with a temporary blessing. It only meant that she needed some deeper work to resolve these issues permanently.

Although the tension and pain were now gone, I still had to pray over her shoulder so that she could raise it overhead. It appeared that it had again physically locked up after six months of tension. She still needed a miraculous work beyond the emotional healing. She found healing again that day and was able to raise her arm overhead without pain. She would not need the surgery that she had planned.

This story is an example of very rapid healing in all these areas, but not everyone moves through issues nearly this quickly. However, this is also an example of process. Nobody resolves all their issues in one prayer session or even a few. Realistically, all of us need to continually make more progress.

Too often, I've run into a mentality among Spirit-filled crowds that we are supposed to be "totally healed" or "totally free," which should happen immediately or even after following somebody's step-by-step program. That type of mindset is religious fantasy, not reality, and a type of sales pitch. People are more likely to buy something that promises spiritual perfection in a single day. These "products" don't require a minister to dig down into the nitty-gritty with anyone, only to perform, take people's money, and move onto the next customer. People are left with a delusion that causes them to resist dealing with their real issues.

I don't think I've ever known anybody who has been "totally free and healed," but everyone can receive more freedom and healing if they are willing to pursue it. I know I am still receiving more. We need persistence and a commitment to go to the root of the issue in the healing process. All these issues: fractured parts, emotional wounds, physical conditions, and more can be interrelated.

People will also make life decisions to go in a different direction and might end up needing to resolve some of the same issues again in the future. Thank God that He is patient with us even when we do this, or we'd all be doomed. We need to reflect this patience with others and be willing to minister to them without condemnation when they are ready to receive again.

Effective Emotional Healing in Memories

I used the following simple approach with Jenn to resolve emotional issues not found in fractured parts:

I rely on the work of the cross and the promises in Scripture of what it accomplishes to liberate us from painful emotions and strongholds. Isaiah 53 says that Jesus "has borne our griefs and carried our sorrows" (NKJV), and John the Baptist preached that He would be "the Lamb of God who takes away the sins of the world." I've found that the Lord will fulfill these true and reliable promises—He will miraculously "take away our sins" and "bear our griefs and sorrows" so that we no longer have to carry them.

To successfully take our "stuff" to the cross, we might first need to learn a few practical lessons. First, we need to let the Lord into the real content of our hearts, which is why I'm going to advise really getting in touch with your emotions and tracing them back to their earliest root in your life.

We also need to get rid of anger, bitterness, and shame before addressing other negative feelings. This is because anger and bitterness put us in prison where we are "handed over to the tormentors" as Jesus said in Matthew 18. Likewise, shame keeps us in bondage because it is a matter of not believing the Gospel in that particular area of our hearts. If we don't believe the Gospel, we miss out on its benefits. Once we let the Lord remove these issues, other painful emotions can typically be removed completely by taking the following steps:

1.   Get in touch with the root of the pain.

Feel the negative emotion that you want to address and resolve, whether fear, powerlessness, low self-esteem, rejection, abandonment, hopelessness, anger, humiliation, etc. You might try to define it in words. Really connect with that emotion.

Now relax, turn off your logical "thinker," and just focus on the emotion. Drift back through that feeling (again, not with your logic or with your opinion of where the issue originated, but only through the emotion) to the first time in your life you felt exactly that same way. You will most likely drift backward through memories until you settle on one memory or on a set of memories at an early age.

Explore this key memory connected to those emotions and try to define what you feel there. Try to connect with what is there emotionally. Don't try to figure it all out. Don't try to understand why you felt the way you did or develop some complex theory of where your problems might have started. Just connect with the emotions at a simple level.

You want to connect with the earliest root of the emotional issue because dealing with it at a later stage will often not be fully effective.

2. Remove any anger.

The good news is that, instead of trying to forgive in our own strength, we can rely on the Lord's promise that He "takes away our sins." Let the Lord supernaturally remove any anger toward others or even toward the Lord himself.

Get in touch with the anger by remembering the incident and feeling the emotions. You do not want to just "jump through forgiveness hoops," parroting empty words without connecting with your heart.

Confess the revengeful emotions as sin or confess holding onto them as sin. Then, renounce them by saying that you don't want them in your life anymore. You must be genuine and sincere with both of these key points. God looks at your heart not just at your words.

Trust the Lord to remove the revengeful emotions and all other painful emotions from the memory based on the work of the cross. Just believe, hand over the emotions, and wait a few seconds for Him to take them.

You might need to command the enemy to go if the feelings don't immediately leave. He might be holding the negative emotions in place. You also might need to take authority and resist the enemy if he is hindering you in other ways, such as shutting down your emotions, blocking off your memories, causing anxiety or distractions, etc.

135

If you still experience some residual anger, don't give up. Repeat the process and trust the Lord to take the rest of it. If any still remains, you might need to trace that anger back to an even earlier memory where it is rooted and go through the process again.

Once you evict the anger, all other negative emotions in the memory will often spontaneously leave as well. The entire issue might be resolved at this point.

3. Remove any shame.

Examine the root memory and check to see if you feel any shame or guilt. If you sense the need, promptly repent of any wrongdoing on your part.

Realize that Jesus died for the sins of the entire world. That includes all the sins of Hitler, every child molester, every serial killer, and whatever you did wrong for which you feel shame or blame. Put your sin in that light, compared to all the sins of the entire world—past, present, and future— for which Jesus died.

Receive the Lord's forgiveness and forgive yourself based on His love and forgiveness toward you.

Now, command the shame to go along with any spirits trying to hold it in place. Give the Lord a few seconds to take the shame. This also might spontaneously resolve other negative emotions in your memory. If not, by this point, you are free from the shame and anger, ready to address the rest of the negative emotions.

4. Trust the Lord to remove all other negative emotions.

He bore your sorrows so that you don't have to. Simply trust Him to take them. You might need to command the enemy to go if he is holding them in place.

Again, if some remain, they often need to be traced to an earlier memory where you will find their true root. Just deal with them in that memory to remove them for good.

Many times, if you cannot connect with the emotions or memories, or if you cannot get them to leave completely, you might be dealing with a fractured part.

Caution: If you work with more severely fractured parts who discover repressed memories, do not try to go into those memories to re-explore them or to feel out the emotions in them as you can cause an "abreaction." This means that you will totally relive the experience of your abuse physically and emotionally just as if it were happening again in real time.

Some forms of traditional counseling have relied on that approach to heal dissociation since it brings up the repressed emotions to a conscious level, breaking down the dissociative barriers in the mind, but obviously, this can be a horrible experience. Instead of emotionally exploring the newly surfaced memory and abreacting, just have the Lord identify the pains and issues in the memory and have the part hand all that over to Him. He will take away the pain and anger, etc. instantly so that you do not have to relive it.

Chapter 19: Matt

Reaching Demonized, Aggressive, Jesus-Hating Parts

So far, we've written about getting in touch with, healing, and integrating fractured parts. We've shared about how the Lord works miraculously in this realm when we invite him to. Still, everything doesn't always go so smoothly.

What about when parts refuse to cooperate, when they are terrified of and unwilling to meet Jesus, when they associate him with the abuse they've suffered? What about when people's parts actively work to sabotage the healing process or even to directly harm the person and other parts within them? What about when you run into what seems like a demon, but no matter what you do, you can't seem to get it to budge an inch? This section will give some answers to these and other questions.

Dan's Story

"Dan" had grown up in an abusive Christian cult that presented God as a raging, punitive monster, waiting to smite anyone who deviated even a little bit from a set of rigid requirements. These "requirements" were all based on a very narrow, literalist, and graceless interpretation of the King James Bible.

Members molded themselves into the image of this "god," terrorizing one another in the Lord's Name. If you were thought to be even slightly disobedient to "God's authority," meaning your parents or higher-ranking members of the cult, they were quick to beat you physically. Dan received constant, vicious beatings in the Name of Jesus that were supposedly aimed at saving him from the wrath of God. Probably even worse things occurred since he had no memory of a large chunk of his mid-childhood years.

As an adult, Dan came to me, asking for healing. He was dealing with overwhelming and irrational fears, suspicions, and out-of-control anger. These emotions were threatening to destroy his marriage. Given his background, I wasn't surprised to learn that most of his fractured parts wanted nothing to do with Jesus or with any traditional representation of the Christian God. At first, they refused to even speak with me.

In our first meeting over the phone, I verbally called out to any fractured parts within Dan, offering healing. I explained that I was not there to force them to do anything they didn't want to do, and neither was Jesus. We were just there to heal them as much as they were willing to receive. Jesus could take away their pain but would not make them participate.

This message usually calms down parts and helps them to feel more comfortable with opening up. Instead, Dan actually felt his parts becoming angry. He heard suspicions and accusations toward me among his parts. Some of the older, leading parts in his system were saying that I was a homosexual.

Dan's cult had more or less taught him that any sin could eventually be forgiven except homosexuality. This was the worst possible accusation that his fractured parts could make.

One part piped up that was willing to talk with me. He wanted to ask me a question. After I agreed, the question came, "Do you have a girlfriend?" When I answered, "No," Dan could hear his parts laughing. Now they were sure that I was a homosexual, an utter abomination! I told them that if they really wanted the truth, they could invite the Lord to meet with them, and they could ask Him if I was homosexual. They weren't biting.

Dan was nice enough to apologize for the way his parts were treating me, but we still didn't seem to be making any progress.

An older part, perceived deep within a house where many of Dan's parts lived, wanted to ask me some more questions. He asked me what I thought about the teachings from his childhood: that God was condemning so many people for their sins and that people would be tortured forever in a fiery hell.

I offered to invite Jesus to come and directly answer these questions, knowing that the Lord would give him the perfect answers as well as lead into healing whatever issues the part was carrying. He refused, saying that he didn't trust Jesus, that he trusted me more, even though that wasn't saying much.

I offered my take on how Jesus came to save the world, not condemn it, and that Jesus is the perfect expression of who God is. Just like Jesus, God is not out to condemn anyone, no matter what they do. In fact, Jesus took all the sin and condemnation of the entire world upon Himself when He went to the cross, revealing a God who is for us even in the midst of our worst sins, looking to redeem us rather than to punish us. I shared that Jesus revealed a God who is completely love, who has no "other side" or "other mood" except love for us as the Scripture says in 1 John 4:8, "God is love."

I shared my understanding from my studies. I've found today's popular view of an eternal, torturous hell to be based on nothing but mistranslations and misinterpretations of Scripture. I found that complex, metaphorical passages of the Bible, besides being mistranslated, have often been overly simplified and taken literally in popular theology, changing the meaning into something that was never intended. In many instances, these kinds of explanations have tended to open up people's parts to a willingness to meet the Lord, so that Jesus Himself could further explain and even personalize His answers to their deepest needs and wounds. Dan's older part listened to me; however, then he receded into the darkness, becoming silent again.

As I continued talking with Dan and reaching out to whoever was in there, one five-year-old part became willing to step up and extend enough trust to speak with me. Dan perceived that he was walking down a long corridor into a room where we could meet, but an older "boss" part was coming to snatch the five-year-old back to where he had come from.

The five-year-old was terrified of this older part and shared with me that it often beat him and the others to keep them under control. I'm not sure how "beating" works within the world of fractured parts since they don't have physical bodies, but several people have shared that their parts consider these beatings to be as real as physical beatings.

I used authority in Christ and commanded the "boss" part, as well as anything else coming to punish the child, to be restrained and unable to nab the five-year-old or to cause him any harm. The child became free to approach me and to speak as the older part apparently retreated.

Dan had great spiritual discernment and tended to know people's hearts to some degree upon meeting them, and he shared with me that this five-year-old was walking in the same gift. He shared that they could both tell I was trustworthy.

Sometimes, those who come from very abusive environments where people used fear and great punishment to keep them under control will internalize their abusers in the form of fractured parts. The purpose of this is to help keep them in line, avoiding punishment from the flesh-and-blood person.

That strategy might have kept them a little safer at the time, but the controlling part now maintains the bondage of fear and punishment long after the original abuse. In dealing with these parts who are perpetuating the abuse within, I've sometimes been able to use a declaration of authority to lock them up in a cage while the other parts were being healed, only letting them out to receive their own healing after the rest were completely safe. In other cases, I've only been able to restrain such troublemakers temporarily.

I find that authority in Christ only works to the degree that the Lord is willing to back it up. If I make a command that He isn't backing, such as trying to lock up a bunch of destructive parts in padded rooms when He is trying to be gentle with them, it won't happen. For example, the parts might be a group of three-year-olds who only want attention and healing. At those times, I find it effective to restrain the parts from causing harm at the moment but not effective to try locking them up in solitary confinement and hiding the key, so to speak.

Back to Dan's story, the boy refused my offer to meet Jesus, afraid that he would be like the "Jesus" of his cult. He wasn't willing to meet with the Father, either, scared that He would turn out to be the punitive monster whom he grew up fearing.

I asked him what he wanted, and he wanted water. By faith, I released water into the room. He began drinking, swimming, playing, and having a great time in the water. The water was doing something deep within him as he merely played in it.

I recognized this as the "Living Water," the Holy Spirit Himself, although I didn't say so out loud. I told the boy that the water could speak to him, asking him if that was okay. He gave his permission, and the water took on the form of a human body, beginning to speak to and minister to the child.

The boy shared that he was afraid of the "boss man" coming in and abusing him again, so I told him that the water could protect him. The child gladly accepted my offer. He could see the water forming around the door to the hallway, sealing off the room so that the mean boss couldn't enter.

Still, the boy was not only afraid but emaciated, like a prisoner of war, in addition to being bruised and scarred from the boss' regular beatings. I asked if he would allow the water to heal him, strengthen him, and to take away his fear. After he agreed, the water took away his fear and trauma, transforming his appearance into a heathy and extremely muscular boy. He said that he was no longer the slightest bit afraid.

The Living Water and the child continued to play with each other. The Living Water indicated that He wanted to be left to spend time with the boy to allow him to have the childhood he had missed during Dan's actual childhood. I had been pressing for more steps of instant healing, leading to integration as soon as possible. Apparently, the Lord thought the boy just needed to play for a while before he was ready for all that.

At times like this, the Lord wants to do even more than healing the parts' traumas. He might want to spend time building up the parts through relationship with Him, giving them time to play and to be loved before integration. Some parts need these sorts of inner voids filled before they are fully healed.

A Walk down the Hall

Dan heard a female voice screaming within him as he received an image in his mind of a demon dragging a naked girl by her hair down a hallway. She continued kicking and screaming for help. I commanded the demons to be restrained and to let the girl go. The screaming stopped. I began to ask if any parts down the hallway would like healing.

Dan became aware that this hallway had rows of doors on each side like a motel, no, more like a prison. Each doorway was sealed with iron bars with fractured parts kept in each room.

We entered one room, which had a demonic-looking dog creature inside that was growling and barking at us. I commanded any demonic aspects of this being to be separated from any true human part of it, declaring that I only wanted to talk to the human aspect and that anything demonic was to be bound up and forbidden to operate. The dog suddenly became two beings.

A man was now on one side of the room and a demon on the other. I received permission from the human part to completely remove the demonic, which left on command. However, now the human part was missing the lower half of his body! I prayed for a restoration of his lower body, which happened instantly.

I've regularly run into parts that were partially human and partially demonic although I have no idea what causes that condition. I've seen what a game changer this approach is in these situations as I command the human aspect to be separated from the demonic and then receive permission from the human aspect to evict the demons.

It isn't always obvious that this is what you are dealing with. Sometimes, you will run into parts who seem ultra-demonized, and this might be what you're facing, or it might not. You might run into something that seems and acts like a demon in every way, but your authority in Christ will have very little effect on it. You might be able to stop some of its most harmful behaviors as with any other fractured part, but you won't be able to cast it out or stop it from mouthing off to you, for instance.

If we know that Jesus gave us "authority over all the power of the enemy" (Luke 10:19), and we believe in that authority enough to use it effectively, we know that it a demon can't resist that authority. It's just not possible. When we run into something that acts like a demon but that can resist authority, we know that it isn't really a demon. In my experience, it is often one of these half-human, half-demon parts that need to be separated into two. Then, when you have permission from the human aspect, authority will work to quickly remove the demonic.

Another possibility is that another human spirit is trapped within the person, being used by the enemy, and in these cases, you might or might not be able to cast it out. Sometimes, these must be delivered and rescued, very much like fractured parts, and many of the same principles apply. I'll share a little more on this subject later.

At times, I've had to just listen to the Lord and pray according to what I was shown since things didn't seem to be working according to my usual understanding. Once, an aggressive being was causing trouble and didn't respond to commands to be bound up or to separate the demonic from the human. I was led to have it lifted up in the air and shaken so that the fractured part inside this being would fall out from within a demonically animated set of clothing. After the fractured part was released in this way, I was able to ask permission to remove the demonic clothes that were controlling him. The aggressive activity then stopped, and the part inside the evil clothes could receive healing.

Back to Dan's story, the name of the part who had just been delivered was "Dogvomit," reflecting a sermon Dan had heard as a kid about people returning to their sins as a dog goes back to its vomit. After this message, one of Dan's elders nicknamed him "Dogvomit." Apparently, this part, now filled with condemnation, had taken its name from that expression.

He didn't want to talk much but wanted protection from the demons and the mean boss who came into the rooms to abuse the parts. I invited the Water to come and form a barrier over the door to his room just as it had done in the boy's room.

"Dogvomit" was glad to be protected from his tormentors. Still, no matter what I said or offered, he didn't want to interact with me. He even refused to have a conversation with the Water. When I asked him what he wanted, he asked for a smoke, so I asked the Water to bring him a cigar. Now, two cigars were sitting in an ashtray on Dogvomit's table where only one had been before— an old one that he had been smoking and the new one that the Lord had brought. That's as far as we progressed that day. I wished that we could have let the Lord give him a new name.

In our next session, we revisited "Dogvomit" and found him to be in pretty much the same condition as he was before. He was enjoying the protection that the barrier of Water provided against demons and the boss part. He was still slowly contemplating the two cigars. He still didn't want to talk, and I could only leave him be again, moving on to other parts to see who might want help.

Dan again heard the little girl screaming, and he became aware of her in another room on another floor of this building. She was screaming in pain as she was raped by a demon. I commanded the demon to stop and sought the girl's permission to have him removed. He was then removed instantly with a simple command.

I introduced myself to the girl, and she shared that her name was "Rape." I asked if she would like Jesus to come to her, protect her, and heal her. She angrily answered "No!" I asked if she would like the Water to come and help her, which was again met with an emphatic "No!"

I suggested that a woman, an animal, or even a teddy bear could come and help her. This time, instead of a simple "no," she began striking out. Dan felt the strikes causing damage to his core self. She was forced to stop at my declaration of faith as I put up a barrier so that she would no longer be able to cause Dan any harm. When she calmed down, I asked her who she wanted to come and help her. She shared that she wanted another little girl, someone like her.

Soon, a knock came at her door, and as it opened, a little girl who looked just like her was on the other side. Her name was "Whole," and she radiated love. "Rape" let "Whole" into her room and began to receive comfort and ministry from her. After a few minutes, "Whole" walked "Rape" out of her room and into a passageway of light, where she disappeared, becoming instantly healed and integrated on the spot.

You can commonly find fractured parts of the opposite gender from the host. Many women will have male Protector parts, and men will have female parts carrying pain and other emotions. As the parts receive healing, I've always seen the Lord change them back into the same gender as their host at some point before integration even though, in this case, we didn't see that happen.

Another unusual aspect here was how the Lord chose to heal and integrate "Rape" in one fell swoop by just walking her into the light. I've rarely seen Him do this but have observed it from time to time.

Usually, He walks them through many individual steps of healing before taking them "into the light" for integration. I'm not sure why He is able to do the quick version in some instances but not in others, but I imagine it must have something to do with the condition of the part or the state of their will.

I'm pretty sure that "Rape" was created from a real instance of rape although that wasn't revealed in the session nor did Dan ever share any related experience. At the very least, he might have had a spiritual encounter that involved a demonic rape as was continuing to happen to this part. Notice that the Lord didn't bother uncovering any memories belonging to this girl even though she might have held some memories of which Dan had no knowledge. He just healed her. I also didn't bother to say anything to Dan about where the part might have come from.

Dan's Eagle Identity

Not only can people's parts and Core Identities (Guardian, Function, Emotion) be the opposite gender due to some manner of brokenness, but they can also be animals as well. After the previous progress with Dan, he still wasn't feeling like his anger, suspicion, and fear issues had left. They were still threatening to destroy his marriage. I began praying with him again, and we ran into his Guardian. He saw it in the form of a giant wooden eagle that was eating dead rotten flesh, barfing it back up, then eating it again.

The eagle, with its great eyesight, was a picture of Dan's discernment. I believe his Guardian was in this form because Guardians focus on discernment and on deciding who to trust. The rotten flesh he was eating turned out to be bitterness and accusations on which he was feeding, producing jealousy and anger.

When a person walks in such sharp discernment as Dan does, they are easier to pray with in this way because they tend to have less of a struggle with awareness of what is happening spiritually within them. They see clearly in visions and hear the Lord's counsel loudly. On the other hand, Dan's background of heavy trauma and religious abuse made his healing process much more complicated than the average person's. A person like him might be ideal for training if you are moving from beginning to more advanced levels of inner healing and deliverance ministry.

I first offered this "Guardian" eagle some better food, which materialized in front of him in the spiritual realm as a meal on a silver platter. As he hopped over to the wholesome food and began eating, we introduced the Lord, who had ultimately given it to the eagle. As the eagle jumped on Jesus' arm and began to trust Him, Dan suddenly felt that he could now trust Jesus at a significantly higher level. A few more eagles seemed to come out of nowhere and started jumping on Jesus' arm. I believe that these were also fractured, "Protector" parts that had splintered from the original Guardian eagle.

Jesus began feeding and healing them all, and a whole flock of eagles suddenly showed up to befriend him and to receive the good food from Him. A group of baby eagles even showed up to crawl all over Jesus, examining Him. As all the eagles were fed and healed, Jesus finally put each of them inside the first eagle, a picture of the fractured Protector parts integrating into the core Guardian that was still made of wood. He then offered the wooden eagle back to Dan to put inside himself. This was a picture of the Guardian identity synchronizing with other aspects of Dan's core.

Before going further, I need to give you an explanation of the difference between integration and synchronization is in order here. Integration means that a fractured part has been restored to the core person, losing its old identity and becoming part of the core identity.

Synchronization, as I use the term, refers to an identity who was originally created to be a fully functioning identity within itself being restored to unity with others of the same kind. The identity was out of alignment from the rest of the God-ordained identities within a person, but again joins the group to fulfill their unique role in the context of the team which makes up that person, somewhat like how the Trinity operates.

A synchronized identity can still function independently and can still be called out and ministered to from time to time before returning to their role among the whole. A truly integrated identity will not be called out again and ministered to in the future because they were never meant to be an independent identity in the first place. They lose their independent identity upon integration.

Back to the encounter with Dan and his Guardian eagle, I asked if Jesus wanted to finish healing up this eagle before full synchronization. He apparently did because He took out some sandpaper, sanded off his rough edges, and turned him into a pure gold eagle. The now literally golden eagle flew into Dan's chest, and they became one, in unity, or "synchronized."

Dan, who had so many trust issues toward God and everyone else before this experience, expressed an entirely new level of trust and peace, especially toward the Lord. He began to have an experience of God's nearness and affection in his daily life at a much higher level. I believe this was a matter of his Guardian Identity being healed and synchronized along with all these fractured "Protector parts" (the other eagles) being healed and integrated during the same prayer session. He found that the suspicion, anger, and a large part of the fear he had originally sought help with had vanished.

He later told me of the large building full of rooms containing parts, such as "Dogvomit," "Boss," and the five-year-old, spontaneously integrating and disappearing from within him. Somehow, the Lord seemed to do a tremendous work over a short time after only coming into the building as the Living Water and having the opportunity to begin helping a few of the parts. The healing of the Guardian identity and the various Protector parts might have led to his system opening up to such spontaneous healing on its own.

We'll come back to the rest of Dan's story later in the book.

Maggie's Lion Story

Maggie was highly dissociative when I met her. She clearly switched from personality to personality while speaking with me. Some of her identities claimed that they had no reason to believe they had any fractured parts, that they only needed to know their identity in Christ and all would be well. Another personality told me that they knew they had DID and needed help.

Some personalities were mature adults, arguing the case theologically that there was no biblical evidence for fractured parts while other personalities curled up on the floor in a fetal position, claiming to be small children trapped in a room, experiencing overwhelming fear, pleading to be "let out of here." When one part of Maggie surfaced, she tended to have no awareness of any of the other ones.

I'm not a doctor, and neither was Maggie, so neither of us were qualified to diagnose her with DID. At the same time, I think a psychologist would most likely have diagnosed her as such. The level of dividedness she experienced was on a totally different level from any of the other folks that I've shared about up to this point.

Her fractured parts and the symptoms she lived with were much more dramatic than those of other clients, which I think indicated a completely different situation, such as DID or another serious dissociative disorder rather than only common fractured parts/fragments. Still, the Lord could heal her in the same ways as He had healed the others.

Some of Maggie's personalities were strong believers in Jesus while others hated the mention of His name. These parts' experience was that all the preaching over several decades had been empty promises resulting in no relief from their torment. Where was Jesus when you needed Him? Where was the supposed healing and freedom? They sure weren't experiencing it.

As these personas would "Rolodex" between one another throughout our conversations, I could only listen and try my best to follow, ministering something life-giving to each one who was willing to receive. More often than not, my attempts were clumsy at best.

Still, during our prayer times over the coming weeks, the Lord rescued fractured parts from emotional states of torment and terror, from houses with scary demons and dark portals hidden in closets, from rooms with abusers threatening to come in at night, from a landscape with witchcraft spirits in the woods, and so on. Many of her parts were brought to a new place of freedom and peace. People's parts commonly need rescuing from some form of spiritual captivity inside such structures within the person's internal world. These were only a few examples.

Usually, if you find a fractured part, you can probably assume that the Lord wants to remove it from its original location. Even if the parts are found in a seemingly innocuous place, such as their childhood home, this will typically be a place of bondage, a place representing the stronghold of their original wounding. They will not be healed or free until they escape.

With most people, I've usually invited Jesus to come in, heal the parts, and lead them out of their places of captivity to a new, safe place where they can either rest or immediately move further into healing and full integration. In Maggie's case, her parts struggled with the idea of Jesus coming to them. They had been abused so heavily by people that most of them didn't trust anything coming to them in the form of a person.

Many of her parts needed to encounter Jesus in the form of a spiritual being of light or as an invisible sense of peace rather than as a man. At other times, one of Maggie's parts needed to go into a place of captivity where another part was held and lead that one out. Sometimes, they needed me to pray for them and to use declarations of faith to release them from their pains and their bondages because they didn't trust the other parts of Maggie to relate to them.

One of Maggie's fractured parts was expressing to me how she felt horribly uncomfortable and distrusting of people. This part had not spoken to another person for almost her entire life. She had been walled up within Maggie for so long, carrying tremendous loneliness. Maggie became aware of a deep pain of loneliness and rejection whenever this part's emotions filtered to the surface.

I asked if we could invite Jesus to meet with her and to be her friend so that she wouldn't need to be lonely anymore, but she hated that idea. She was afraid to allow another human into her personal space since all this part had known from humans was abuse and rejection. She was deeply afraid of being rejected.

I told her that the Lord could come to her in any form she wanted, and she decided she was willing to meet Him if he came as an animal. She began to laugh as she saw a lion approaching her. She literally, physically felt as if a huge, invincible lion were standing next to her in her home, and that nothing could harm her. As the lion snuggled with her, her fears of rejection and abuse lifted, and she began to exclaim how much more wonderful it was to have a lion as a friend than even a human version of Jesus. She felt so peaceful and protected.

Another part came to the surface, expressing anger and hatred toward people. She wanted the lion to bite everybody. I wasn't able to minister to that part beyond just listening to it that day, but Maggie shared with me that she felt this was progress in itself. In the past, she had internalized this anger, which led her to suicide attempts, but now this part of her was able to express it for what it truly was, anger toward humanity.

Maggie was also able to be "co-conscious" with this part, which was another evidence of progress. In the past, she might be aware of her normal personality or of this angry part at a given time, but now she was able to hold the awareness of both personalities at once. Maggie was now giving this angry part of her a voice, rather than shutting it down within as she always had before. In and of itself, this was huge progress.

Overall, Maggie seemed to be doing much better. Her daily emotional states were becoming a lot more stable. Her most overwhelming pains didn't seem to be with her anymore. She had a stronger sense of self and was able to set boundaries with others more effectively. Although the signs weren't completely gone, she was showing fewer signs of heavy dissociation. She was beginning to believe that what we had been doing was working.

Maggie sent me a message late at night before our next scheduled session. Actually, her angry part did. She wrote that ministering to her was just a waste of time, that nothing we'd done had worked at all. She said that she was back to square one and feeling tormented again with the same issues she always had.

I tried to encourage her that these symptoms were only another wounded part coming to the surface and that we could see healing for that part just the same as we had for the previous ones.

Often, during the healing process, people will experience issues very similar to what was previously healed in the past resurfacing. They will often think their problems and bondages "came back." With fractured parts, though, many parts might have the same or similar issues, and after some parts are healed, more will often surface, looking for the same kind of healing, too. Bondages and wounds don't just "come back" to anyone unless they willfully allow them back. The enemy has no power but what we give him. She didn't believe my explanation and wasn't afraid to say so.

I tried to share something with her about inviting the lion to help her, but she immediately shot it down. "Blah, blah, blah. Don't talk to me about Jesus. He never does anything for me! I don't believe in that stuff." I was disturbed by this sudden change from beginning to believe in the healing process to total, hardened disbelief. However, this turned out to be just another sign of progress.

This angry part of Maggie, so used to being shut down and totally denied a voice, was being given an opportunity to boldly speak her mind for the first time. These issues were indeed coming to the surface so that they could be processed and healed.

During our session the next day, Maggie was sharing that she could hear a part of herself screaming in terror, the same part she had heard screaming in her head for many years. She woke up at night with extreme anxiety, shaking, aware of the state this part constantly lived in, and she did her best to suppress it all so that she could function in her daily activities. This screaming part turned out to be tied to the angry part. The anger was apparently due to the fact that the terrorized one was not receiving any help.

When Maggie started trying to minister to these parts on her own that morning, they weren't willing to have anything to do with her. A lot of self-hatred was involved. Some of this was due to the fact that the parts had been shut down within and had not been listened to for so long. The Lord had spoken to Maggie and given her a strategy for healing long ago, to "love yourself." She had doubted that message and hadn't practiced it toward these parts.

In the session, I invited the angry part to speak. She shared that she could still hear the tormented one screaming in terror. The angry one wanted to use Maggie's own fist to punch her in the face for not listening, overwhelmed with hatred. I restrained the demonic from this part and then asked if I could remove all demons along with the self-hatred. Once the part gave me permission and I followed through commanding those things to go, Maggie's anger suddenly subsided. She didn't want to punch herself anymore.

Though the hatred was now gone, she still didn't know what love was since she hadn't experienced it. She felt empty inside. She wanted Jesus to meet with her but not as the lion. She said she felt like the lion was a cop-out; she wanted to know Jesus as a human person for the first time.

When we invited Jesus, she felt a sense of peace come over her as Maggie's parts often had, but no person was showing up to talk to her. In hindsight, I think this part wasn't really ready to meet Jesus the man, although she had a certain desire to do so. I've found that Jesus will show up to the degree to which parts are truly comfortable receiving Him. Sometimes, they aren't even aware of how different the state of their heart is from that of their words.

I asked if I could pray for Jesus to reveal His love to this part, and something began pulling her back. She felt tied up. This is a common way that the demonic will interfere when they still have a place within the person due to the part's agreement when one of their key strongholds is threatened. I've found parts to begin to be dragged away, even hidden somewhere, or to have chains, cords, or bands tighten around their throats or lungs to stop them from speaking. These activities must be stopped by a command of faith. The issue giving them a foothold must sometimes be revealed and resolved before the attack can be removed.

This time, I asked the part if I could invite the lion in to talk to her to help her remove whatever was still binding her. She responded, "But what if something worse happens?" Only knowing a lifetime of demonic torment with no relief, no matter who preached or prayed over her for years, this part was afraid that even if we did manage to get rid of the bondage, something worse would inevitably take its place. She expressed her belief that the enemy was really big and that God could do very little for her. After all, she was the part who had messaged me earlier.

She hadn't seen much positive, only lots of evil happening in her world. Her spiritual discernment allowed her to see into the lives of many others and to see the bondage in which they were living. She was aware of so many who lived in torment without ever seeming to find freedom. Evil appeared to be really powerful. She expressed feeling disqualified by her unbelief from receiving God's help even if He could somehow help her.

I tried to share that freedom didn't depend on if she believed enough but that I could pray for her and that the Lord would reveal how big He is. He would help her believe if she only gave Him permission to try.

The part continued arguing, sharing that she had a feeling that some aspect of her was unredeemable, that some part of her was so captured by the enemy that it couldn't possibly be rescued, no matter what. She had seen parts of herself and so many other people trapped in a hell realm, a realm of unspeakable torture. How could God be good if He allows parts of all these people to remain trapped in hell? How can He possibly rescue her if He allows so many others to remain trapped? Rescuing her and leaving all of them would be the greatest travesty of all.

How can it be right that even children are trapped in realms of hell and suffering? What have they done wrong? How can it be that she sees eighty-year-old people with parts of themselves still trapped in hell at the end of their lives just because they are broken people? If Jesus isn't rescuing them, how can He be trusted? She demanded an explanation before she was willing to receive His help.

I explained that God didn't allow that or have anything to do with it, as I've observed Him explain to person after person who demanded answers about their tragedies, but that people are trapped in those realms through their choices and the choices of those in their generational lines. However, Jesus rescues those who give Him permission to do so. I explained that Jesus goes where He is invited and will rescue all who allow Him to rescue them.

Many times, it is better to allow the Lord to come and answer such questions Himself because He does a better job of it, but it isn't always wrong to share what He has revealed before. She was satisfied with my answer enough to become willing to invite the Lord to show up in whatever form was needed to help her with her fear and unbelief.

This hopelessly unbelieving part of Maggie suddenly had a sense of herself transforming into a lion. This time, Jesus hadn't only come as a lion but was revealed as a lion within her! All her fear and unbelief instantly left, and she now felt that she could do absolutely anything. Experiencing oneness with God, she was ready to charge into all the rooms of hell where her child parts were being held in captivity to rescue them from those places, knowing that nothing could stop her.

Her experience as the lion was so profound that she became physically aware of the tremendous weight of her lion body and could feel the texture of her fur. She found that she could use her imagination to move her body through the realms of time, space, and spiritual dimensions at a naturally impossible rate of speed. She was going to hell to rescue all the children under her care, and she would tear apart any demon that stood in her way.

"Am I making all this up?" she asked. "I can feel myself as a lion, but I don't even believe in this kind of thing! Is this really happening?" An adult part of her who previously denied the existence of her fractured parts and the validity of her spiritual experiences was now speaking, even as the lion traveled through spiritual dimensions.

As one part of her was aware of being the lion, another part of her was simultaneously aware of petting the lion and examining all its various textures, while at the same time, yet another part of her could see the lion from a second-hand perspective as it ran through black corridors, knocking down steel doors to access trapped children in many rooms. She was aware of a light attached to her as she ran so that she could see in the pitch-black darkness.

Moving at an incredible rate of speed, she knocked down every barrier and invaded every room where child parts had been screaming in horror while trapped in torturous cages. She allowed them to climb on her back as she raced to the next room and the next child. Once she had all of the many children, she carried them to a place of safety in another realm. She had not only brought her own parts out of this realm of hell, but she seemingly freed all the parts of other people who were trapped in that same location just as she had earlier expressed her sense of injustice at the possibility of her rescue while other people's parts were left behind.

The lion took all the children to a place with a purple river and ultra-green grass where they could rest. Trees had food hanging from them waiting for the children. Everything was alive and inviting, and she had a sense that it was all even more and better than it appeared. This was a place of life and goodness opposite the realm of suffering and death where these parts had existed before.

The lighting was dark enough not to overwhelm these children who had been used to living in pitch-blackness but also bright enough to begin transitioning them to a better realm. As the children's eyes adjusted, the light was steadily increasing. The kids were tired and were going to nap first, and when they awoke, they were invited to jump into the cleansing river and to eat from the life-giving trees.

So many children were now rescued and lay on the grass. None of them were wearing any clothes yet, making it obvious that their healing process was incomplete.

As I've shared before, the clothing of the parts is very important. The Lord doesn't leave any of them naked or in tattered rags. He will bring them to a place of being clothed in all white. Any colors besides white, even for shoelaces, accessories, belt buckles, underwear, or any other article of clothing typically represents problems that need healing, repentance, or deliverance. At times, other colors might be allowed, but these exceptions must be authorized by the Lord Himself.

We see hints of all this in Scripture, where the book of Revelation speaks of people being spiritually naked and needing to be clothed in white garments, of the overcomers dressed in white robes, having been cleansed by the blood of the Lamb. In Isaiah, the Lord said that all our righteousness is as filthy rags, and "though your sins are as scarlet, they will be as white as snow." In Zechariah, the high priest was clothed in filthy garments as he stood in the spiritual realm, and when the Lord cleansed him, he was given a new change of clothes.

The water of life is God's presence, often showing up as a river, spring, or some other body of water. The Lord sometimes leads parts to a hot spring or hot tub of Living Water to soak in so that they can receive healing and cleansing at a slow and relaxed pace over many days. I've regularly begun speaking such hot tubs of Living Water into parts' realms for them to soak in as part of my ministry.

Chapter 20:

Will The Real Jesus Please Stand Up?

Michael: Encountering False Jesuses

When going through the inner healing and deliverance process, I have often encountered false Jesuses—and discovered this to be true for both for myself and others.

An example of a false Jesus is one who harms you, lies to you, or whose face shifts into a demonic form. 2 Corinthians 11:14 says, "And no wonder, for Satan himself masquerades as an angel of light." Demons can disguise themselves in a variety of forms, which often happens when working with very young parts because they might not have ever met the real Jesus. When the enemy comes in and appears as a false Jesus, they can poison the young part's view of God and keep him or her in fear of the only One who can set them free.

I found this to be true a decade ago, long before I even believed in these different parts as these false Jesuses appeared during my inner healing prayer sessions. Nothing has changed since. The most difficult part about a false Jesus is identification. The gift of discernment helps with this, but if the being in question doesn't say or do something to reveal him/herself, there is no real way to know. However, they generally do not hide for very long, and during the prayer sessions, they tend to reveal themselves sooner or later.

One of the most effective ways to deal with a false Jesus is to teach and empower the part with which you are working. As you share with the part what Jesus is actually like and encourage him or her to take authority over every version of Jesus who doesn't treat them with kindness and love, and as they learn that they can make those false ones go away, they will only be further encouraged and empowered to step into maturity—something all young parts need.

Matt: Frank, A Nasty False Jesus, and Dealing with Counterfeits

At the beginning of the session, I saw one of Dan's fractured parts who looked a lot like how I imagined the Gadarene demoniac would look. He was very angry, fearful, unkempt, and wild-eyed.

Dan saw him pacing back and forth in a cave where he lived. This "Gadarene caveman" was raging and smashing things left and right in his wild, demon-inspired anger. Dan suddenly became aware that this part's name was Frank.

I asked Frank why he was so angry. He answered that he was angry about how he looked and about his condition, all cut up and deformed.

I commanded the demonic to be bound and restrained and to be prevented from controlling or influencing him, and Frank instantly calmed down. After I asked for his permission to remove all of the demonic and then issued a simple command for it to "Go," we noticed further improvement in his condition.

I asked Frank if we could invite Jesus into the cave to talk with him. He said "Okay," but held out two daggers, warning that Jesus had better be careful. A shining and robed being began walking into the cave. The closer he came to Frank, the weaker Frank became. He could no longer hold the daggers and simply dropped them to the ground.

As this brilliant being approached Frank, he gave Frank a side hug, and Frank began to melt into his arms. Frank was feeling very weak now, unable to even hold himself up. The being, who appeared to be Jesus, began to change into Frank's likeness with all of his scars, sickliness, and various deformities.

I was becoming very suspicious of this being. I asked Frank to look into his eyes to check if he could see love in them. Instead of eyes, this being only had empty sockets. Staring into the empty sockets, Frank saw pitch-black darkness and sensed creepiness. Obviously, this was not Jesus.

I've found many such spiritual impostors with empty black sockets instead of eyes, but I have also encountered other variations. Some have had crazy eyes, cold eyes, mean or angry eyes, even determined, passionate eyes, but they still lacked love.

Some deceivers had positive qualities in their eyes, such as kindness or calmness, but they appeared with the negatives previously mentioned. Although other beings might appear like Jesus in every way and might even radiate warmth, light, peace, or other such positive qualities, you can tell their true nature by their eyes. Only the true Jesus will have love in His eyes. You will only see positive qualities there with nothing negative.

I asked for Frank's permission to remove the false Jesus and cast him out of the cave. Frank was lying on the ground now, so weak he was near the point of death. This false Jesus had taken all the life out of him during their embrace.

I asked him if I could invite the true Jesus in and this time, make sure that it wasn't a counterfeit. I made a declaration that any false Jesus would be consumed by the Holy Spirit upon even trying to enter the cave. Immediately, Dan saw a wall of flames surround the cave and about ten counterfeit Jesuses, who were already waiting outside to pull the same trick as the last one, burst into flames.

Frank was worried that another false Jesus would enter again but felt that he had no choice but to try. He was at the point of death and needed help. I offered food to strengthen him before we invited another person into the cave.

As I prayed for the food, two birds came in with different kinds of food. A black crow brought some rotten meat, and beside it, a white dove brought some healthy-looking food. Apparently, Dan had become infested with many false Jesuses and false Holy Spirits when he had grown up in the Christian cult, which explained why Frank, his fractured part, was having such a difficult time with counterfeits.

Frank shoved aside the rotten meat and ate the healthy food instead. He began to gain strength. He also wanted water, which I declared brought to him as well. Water now appeared in front of him, strengthening and refreshing him as he drank. When I commanded all counterfeit, rotten food to be consumed by the Holy Spirit, Dan reported that he saw massive stockpiles of food burst into flames from inside the cave.

I called for the true Jesus to come into the cave and minister to Frank, declaring that no false Jesus was allowed to go near him. Dan began to see a wider view of the landscape around Frank's cave, and a huge crowd of maybe 100 or more false Jesuses gathered outside. They all parted to allow the true Jesus to enter the cave. The crowd of counterfeits hissed spitefully at the true Jesus as he walked through their midst, but they couldn't stop him.

I made sure that Frank looked into this Jesus' eyes to check for love. He could see tremendous peace and warmth in Jesus' eyes, and nothing bad at all, and I was sure that this was the true Jesus. He ministered to Frank, walking him through dealing with a variety of personal issues and expressing love to him in various ways until he was totally healed, clothed in all white. We had all the false Jesuses consumed by the fire of Holy Spirit, and they evaporated into smoke in Dan's vision. Frank was led out of his cave into the broad daylight with no more need to hide.

Matt: A Well-Known Leader Freed from Several False Jesuses

Speaking of false Jesuses, I once prayed with a long-time ministry leader who was going through some gut-wrenching trials. His Guardian shared that he was angry with the Lord for only giving him promises in his situation but never actually doing anything to help him. He was going through the most difficult situation in his life, yet all he seemed to hear from the Lord were empty words.

This can be a sign of a false Jesus. A good number of them will sometimes imitate the Lord's promises but just won't follow through. If "Jesus" is promising healing, promising to take away issues and pains, etc., but none of this ever happens, this is a strong sign of an impostor.

I asked this man's Guardian if we could ask Jesus about his concern and if he wanted to express how he felt to the Lord and find some answers. Guardian agreed to that, and I encouraged him to express everything that was on his heart, to lay out all his feelings on the table. I've found that deeply sharing our hearts with the Lord creates an opening for Him to share His heart and wisdom with us in a helpful way.

He expressed how frustrated he was with how much he was suffering and how God seemed to be all words and no power in his situation. He voiced how hurtful it was for him to experience this abandonment. He did receive a reply, a voice telling him to just continue holding on, but he didn't feel that this reply was helpful or comforting in any way.

Since Guardian wasn't seeing this Jesus but was only hearing a voice, I asked him if we could invite this Jesus to reveal himself visually so that we could check his eyes and see if he truly was Jesus. This took a bit of persistence and praying for exposure, but pretty soon, the Guardian did see who this Jesus was—not a living Jesus, but only a painted fresco of Jesus on a wall.

This can be how the "Jesus" of traditional religion shows up: just a picture of Jesus or a relic of Jesus, such as a wooden man on a crucifix or maybe even a religiously ornate, gaudily dressed man who is more of a namby-pamby figure with no power. I had this leader and his Guardian identity renounce the ungodly religious traditions of the denomination he grew up in as well as those from the denominations of his ancestors. The lifeless fresco of Jesus vanished from his vision after he did so. I've frequently found it necessary to have someone renounce religious or occult activities on behalf of not only themselves but also of their ancestors in order to evict fake Jesuses.

We invited the true Jesus to come in and meet with Guardian, and this time, a robed man appeared with fire in his eyes. I urged Guardian to really look in the eyes to discern what character qualities were there. I wanted him to see if he could find love in the fiery eyes of this Jesus.

Guardian told me that he could see intense purpose and determination in these eyes but not love. He began to see that this "Jesus" had a self-willed agenda. He exclaimed, "It's the Charismatic Jesus!"

I had him renounce all the religious spirits and practices he'd picked up from the Charismatic churches, and this Jesus disappeared.

We invited the true Jesus in once more. This time, a floating, robed being, clothed in white showed up, and bright light was shining from him in all directions. This being radiated hope and warmth, but his facial features were obscured. This concerned me because the false ones will often try to hide their eyes to hide their true nature.

I asked the Lord to reveal his eyes if it was Him, and I commanded the eyes to be revealed if it was an impostor. This minister's Guardian identity was suddenly able to see the eyes, and he told me, "I know love is there, but I don't feel it. Why don't I feel the love?" When I had him ask this being why he didn't feel the love, it replied, "Because you don't believe me."

"That doesn't make any sense," answered the minister. He couldn't see any love in the eyes. He only had a sense from them that he was supposed to know that love was there. This was the 'Word of Faith' Jesus!

After religious spirits from the Word of Faith movement were renounced, this Jesus disappeared also. Finally, the real Jesus showed up to meet with the Guardian. Love was immediately evident coming from this one's eyes, and He brought real comfort and healing rather than only speaking empty words.

It might seem like I'm picking a fight with different denominations or movements. This is not to say that everything in these organizations and movements is bad and should be renounced. On the contrary, I believe that these movements offer many important positive attributes to the Body of Christ. The point is simply that, like all large institutions and movements made up of imperfect people, some unhealthy religious traditions were in place, and this man's heavy involvement with these groups invited the wrong spirits into his life. In my experience, no denomination or major religious movement is exempt from this issue. Also, not all "religious tradition" is necessarily evil. I am simply referring to traditions of men which don't truly come from the Lord or do not lead people into real relationship with Him.

At times, you will need to persist until all the imposters truly leave when they show up one after another and require the renunciation of specific spiritual or religious agreements that the person, their parts, or their ancestors have entered into. At times, you can ask a part's permission to remove the trickster, and that will be enough to remove them successfully. Other times, as in this case, the person will need to make a specific renunciation before the impostors will go.

When someone comes from a significant background in the occult or from a family with a serious history of strong and unresolved occult activity in their generational line, I've sometimes found a need for even more persistence than in this case. If you just continue, using personal and generational renunciations to resolve the reasons why each deceiver has a foothold, you will find every last counterfeit spirit removed until you reach the true Jesus, with eyes of love, who comes to minister to the part.

Not only is this worth doing for the fact that the parts are getting delivered from each deceiving spirit who shows up in place of Jesus, but each encounter removes the obstacles that prevent the part from knowing the Lord in a direct, personal way. When He does show up, He will be able to minister to them on a very deep level and begin leading them the rest of the way into healing.

It might seem strange to some that counterfeits would be able to repeatedly show up even when a believer invites Jesus and that the part must walk through renunciations before the counterfeits stop getting in God's way, but it comes down to the Lord respecting our will. When a part of us has chosen to put another spirit in place of him, in a place of worship or religious covenant, such as often occurs with occult practices, false religions, and "Christian" religious activities, the true Jesus will not violate the part's will and just barge into that place until that part comes out of those agreements. It's not that He can't do it, but that He won't renege on the gift of free will and personal authority that He has given us.

Matt: Parts of Dan's Spirit

Once we had freed Frank from the cave, we asked for his help in locating and freeing a part of Dan's spirit who was trapped in a cage. We had previously seen this part during another prayer time. Frank quickly led us to its location.

We had seen several caged parts of Dan's spirit before and were able to release one of them from captivity through a very quick prayer, yet the other was not freed so easily.

Dan felt a bit strange when he saw a vision of the Lord leading the main portion of his spirit and the newly freed fractured part of it in a wedding ceremony, joining them together as one spirit again. He wondered if this imagery meant that he was now marrying himself. How could that be right?

Though I have never seen that imagery before or since, I assured Dan that this was the spiritual realm and that marriage was, in fact, created as an expression of a deeper divine truth, the truth that we become one with God in a spiritual love relationship through the new covenant. God is a Spirit and the originator of the higher spiritual truth that physical marriage foreshadows, so a part of Dan's spirit going through a marriage ceremony to become one again with the whole wasn't far-fetched in my book. It was just an unusual way of looking at it.

Frank had led us to the remaining captive, fractured part of Dan's spirit, which now appeared as a frozen statue to him. As I asked the

Lord to minister to this part of Dan's spirit, to heal him and bring him out of his cage, a giant translucent arm reached down from the heavens above, pouring oil all over it. Dan watched in his mind's eye as this oil turned this part of his spirit from a frozen statue into a little dot with tremendous life inside. So far, this imagery seemed positive. I'd never seen a counterfeit spirit do anything like this. The giant arm from the heavens then picked up the dot, put it into a treasure box, and stuffed the treasure box in a cave with many other treasure boxes haphazardly strewn about.

This seemed very suspicious to me. Why would God stuff part of Dan's spirit into a box and toss it into a cave? The Lord wants to free, heal, and integrate our parts, not place them in further captivity. I quickly commanded any demonic counterfeits involved to be bound up and exposed. I've found that, besides checking the eyes, using a command of authority in Christ can also effectively expose counterfeits.

The ground underneath the cage began to shake, and a massive evil spirit came into view, appearing as a large principality. Half of its body was deep underground and colored like the earth while the other half rose into the heavens, appearing translucent and heavenly. The translucent arm of this giant principality had "ministered" to Dan's fractured part and stuffed it in a cave, not the Lord.

I commanded this thing to be removed and sent to judgment, and we both watched as innumerable warring angels came upon the scene, swarming around this evil principality like thousands of bees. They carried it away so that it could no longer work to deceive and hold this part of Dan's spirit captive. We might have had trouble freeing this part through a quick, simple prayer of declaration during our previous session because it first needed to be delivered from this principality.

By faith, we went to the cave where Dan's part had been stuffed among so many treasure chests. I again relied on a declaration of authority in Christ, commanding all the chests to open, the part of Dan's spirit to be cleansed and removed from all captivity, and all that was good within the chests to be restored to Dan but all that was evil to be consumed by the fire of Holy Spirit.

Dan watched as the treasure chests were opened and the contents of all but one were completely consumed by fire. All that remained was the originally fractured part of Dan's spirit, still appearing in the form of a little dot. Frank seemed to know where this dot belonged, and he directed us to a foreboding castle within Dan's interior world. He informed us that the dot belonged within another fractured part of Dan, who was trapped within this castle.

In an earlier session, we had found a part of Dan who looked like a little red cartoon heart. The little heart had legs and an arrow stuck through its center, just like the classic image of a "wounded heart." According to Frank, this wounded heart lived inside the foreboding castle, and the dot belonged in its center where the arrow was lodged.

When we first met the cartoon heart, Dan sensed that it was very energetic, full of zeal for life and adventure, but surrounded by heavy darkness. Whenever we approached, it ran away from us in fear, using its quick little legs. A prayer to restrain the demonic was necessary to calm the heart enough so that it could talk with us for a bit.

Unlike most parts who gladly accept an offer of freedom after their demons are restrained, the little heart refused. It struggled with great fear and had made an agreement with the darkness, allowing the demonic to insert the arrow through it as the price of "protection."

When I asked how it felt to have the arrow stuck through it, the heart shared that it didn't feel a thing, although it knew that this arrow

173

caused Dan's core personality to live with significant emotional torment along with pain in his physical body. I knew that Jesus would be glad to remove the arrow along with all the demons and offer the little heart much more effective protection than the darkness ever could, but nothing I shared seemed to convince him of this.

With Frank's input about the "dot" belonging where the arrow now lodged, the pieces of the puzzle were starting to fall into place. This heart was separated from the element of Dan's spirit which it had contained, and this part of the spirit was given over to captivity as a second cost of being pierced by the arrow.

This is an example of how I think the "anatomy" of fractured parts typically looks. Though many in this field only talk about "soul fractures" as if these have no impact on our spirits, experience tells me that fracturing also occurs in the spirit. The fractured parts often seem to contain some of our spirit, some of our soul, and are connected to some aspect of our body.

Sometimes, a fractured part might be completely soul or completely spirit, but I think most of them have some aspect of both. Our soul and spirit are meant to be interwoven as one being, not dissociated from one another, so when we form fractured parts, they seem to take an element of both soul and spirit with them.

By faith, we opened the gate and entered the foreboding castle where the little heart lived, wanting a second chance to minister to him. Not surprisingly, the inside of the castle seemed very dark and was filled with demons of fear. Many dark snakes and spiders were crawling around inside. Many beings were in the shadows who might have been parts, so the first thing I prayed was to have all demons pretending to be parts exposed and removed. Every single "part" in this castle suddenly vanished other than the little heart himself.

Many times, demons will impersonate fractured parts and cause all sorts of trouble among the true parts. They might deceive or intimidate the parts or lead them into unholy agreements, etc. In many cases, the true parts involved must break all the agreements made with these "parts" and give the Lord permission to remove them before they will go. In many cases, the impostors must also be exposed for what they are and for their malicious intentions toward the true parts before those true parts will agree to evict them.

The following signs might indicate that a "part" is only a demonic impostor:

- The "part" might be extremely difficult to work with
- The "part" might cause trouble
- The "part" might play along and pretend to receive some healing but will never be fully healed or clothed in all white
- The "part" won't cooperate very well with Jesus, etc.

These signs might also indicate several other things, such as a part-demon, part-human part, a demonically controlled part, a part with another, smaller, very wounded and demonized part living within them, or a part who needs generational cleansing done by the core person before it can be separated from the demonic.

Because of so many possibilities, identifying the demonic impostors through outward evidence is not an exact science. Many demonized parts are wrongly identified as demons by deliverance and healing ministers who make assumptions based on overly simplistic views. I'm not sure there is any way to know for sure which "parts" are demons other than to ask the Lord or to use a command of faith to expose the demons pretending to be parts.

Many times, one or two parts among a group of parts found in some place of captivity or deep darkness are actually demonic impostors. If you can remove them immediately, this can help healing for the true parts to flow much more smoothly. In Dan's case, every other "part" in this castle where the little heart lived turned out to be an impostor.

When I turned my attention to the heart, I had to bind up and restrain the demonic so that he would start talking again. Since the heart wouldn't accept an offer of complete freedom at first, I had to convince him to "try out" freedom from the spirit of fear that had bound him with an agreement that he could have all the fear back if he wanted it.

I've found that if a part isn't willing to completely let the Lord take away their issue, sometimes they are willing to let Him temporarily put it into a nearby box with the agreement that they can open the box and take back the junk if they want it. In this way, they can experience what freedom feels like before they make the decision to let their issue be permanently removed.

I find it necessary to use this approach for anger more often than for any other problem. Many parts carry anger that locks them into other forms of pain and torment, and because they aren't willing to let the Lord remove the anger, they can't be freed from the other emotions either. They might not even believe me when I tell them that they need to remove the anger to get rid of the other problems. The opportunity to experience freedom, under the conditions that they can take back the anger, pain, and torment if they decide they want it back, usually helps them to realize that they are better off without it.

As the heart temporarily laid down the fear, it began to experience what it felt like to be free and quickly gave permission for all fear and darkness to be removed, including the arrow that had been stuck through it for so long.

Jesus ministered to the heart, taking it into His hand, and removed all kinds of wounds and contaminants from it. He took the heart out of the castle. Next, we had the castle destroyed since everything in it was evil. We had the part of Dan's spirit (the dot) put back in the center of the heart where it belonged, and the heart was then put back into the proper spot within Dan. I asked Frank if he wanted to ask anything before he was led into integration, and he only wanted to tell Dan that he loved him.

After Frank was integrated with the other parts we had ministered to up to that point, Dan felt like he had fully received the healing he was looking for and stopped pressing me for any further sessions.

Just as the little heart had shared, the arrow stuck through its center was a source of pain in Dan's body. After the integration, a quick prayer resolved the long-term back pain he had been suffering along with other ailments.

Chapter 21: Diane

Traveling in the Spirit to

Heal Parts

In March 2016, I was ministering to a woman who lived around 60 miles from my home. I traveled there once a week. As I returned home one evening from my weekly trip, my heart was really burdened because we hadn't cleared up the issue that we had been working on. That night, I decided to try an experiment. I traveled in the spirit to her and talked to the fragment that we had been working with earlier. She ended up receiving the Lord that night and going with Him to the garden inside.

I didn't say anything about this to my client. I went to her house the following week, and we worked with a different fragment. This one received the Lord and went with Him to the garden. When my client looked into the garden, she saw two fragments, not just the one.

That excited me! Praying for the fragments in the spirit realm without having the client see it themselves would really help speed up the process. I have tested this a number of times with fairly consistent success. I find it to be a very viable form of ministry. Many times, I travel in the spirit and pray what I see there. I pray for their fragments and see healing happen.

One day, a friend called me, very upset. She felt that her husband was emotionally abusing her, and she asked me to pray. I decided I would try praying in the Spirit and traveling to him. As I went there, a big, mean fragment came to the surface. This fragment was lashing out at her because of the pain he was carrying. I invited the Lord to go to him and heal him and witnessed him doing so. A few weeks later, my friend told me that her husband hadn't been mean to her since the day she asked me to pray.

Now, I was really excited. Her husband would never have let me pray for him. But since fragments have their own will, I can approach them in the spirit realm and ask if they want healing. Most of the time, they do. You can effectively pray this way for your kids, spouse, and other relatives, especially the unsaved.

I have now done this many times with a number of testimonies of behaviors stopping and lives changing. It is a form of intercession and quite an effective form at that.

Healing Core Identities in the Spirit

It was Kathy's second appointment. At the first appointment, we became acquainted and prayed over some generational issues, particularly hatred of women. She had a couple of issues that caused pain in her left leg, and the left side of the body often relates to issues with women while the right side often relates to issues with men. After we prayed, the pain left, and now at our second appointment, she was excited that the pain was still gone. I had decided to pray for her three Core Identities (Function, Guardian, Emotion) at this appointment, hoping that she would receive healing from some of the suppressed emotions she had been carrying for years. One of the biggest results of praying for the three cores at the beginning is often the releasing of suppressed emotions.

I asked the Lord to take me to one of the cores and felt led to start with the Functional Core. As I looked inside, I saw some fragments sitting at desks studying. I felt Kathy was quite intelligent even though she had never voiced that. Her Functional Core came right up to me and said that she wanted the Lord to heal her. This was a first for me. Usually, I first have to talk to the core before it agrees to healing. This was not the case with Kathy's Functional Core; it wanted to be healed immediately. The Lord was able to go inside the core where the functional fragments were located and speak to some of them, healing them as well. Exciting!

As I was planning to go to the next core, I felt led to ask the Functional Core if she wanted to take the Lord to the Emotional Core. She agreed. The Functional Core and the Emotional Core were on great terms. Kathy explained that it felt as if they were best friends. Because Functional took the Lord to Emotional, she quickly agreed to healing and allowed Him to go to some of her fragments as well. Emotion was also willing to give her suppressed emotions to the Lord, releasing the pain she was carrying.

Next, I took the Lord to the Guardian Core, which tends to fight God and wants to do everything on its own. Not so in this case—Guardian quickly came forward to receive the Lord and showed us what was inside—beautiful Protector parts. They loved God and wanted Him. A few remained rebellious and angry, but many more just wanted God to help them.

When we met a week later, Kathy excitedly told me all that had happened the previous week. About three or four hours after our appointment, she started having crying jags, emitting deep sobs with tears pouring down her cheeks. She cried for around five minutes, had a short break, and then went through another jag. This lasted for three hours. Afterwards, she fell asleep and slept all night. She previously never slept more than three hours at a time, so a full night's sleep felt amazing to her. As the week continued, she noticed that she continued to sleep better, sleeping for five to six hours at a time.

She noticed that the tightness she had in her chest area had loosened. She felt like she could breathe better, and the pain in her shoulders was gone.

Two days after praying, she awoke very angry for no reason. She wanted to scream, so she did. She found a safe place and spent some time screaming and shouting. Afterwards, she felt such a release.

Kathy is still on her journey as we pray for individual fragments, but praying for the three cores allowed for healing, which helped increase her faith in God as well as in the process. So much of emotional healing is believing that God is good and that He wants to heal us just as with physical healing. When our faith levels rise, we can receive healing more quickly.

I tend to visit the Core Identities in the spirit realm early on. This gives me a glimpse into what the process of healing will look like. By visiting them and introducing Jesus or Father God to each one, I'll get a sense of who the person is at their core.

I ask the Lord to take me to each one in the order He wants. Sometimes, He starts with the Functional Core. I'll see some aspects of the fragments contained within that one. I'll see how this core is reflected in the person. I always tell the client what I am seeing, and so far, they have always agreed that what I am seeing was true.

When the core receives the Lord along with whatever truth is revealed, I then check to see if that core is okay with the other two cores. Sometimes, a Core Identity might have anger or resentment against another core because of its different responses to situations that the first core thought were wrong. In order to synchronize the cores as a team, they need to be willing to work together.

After those issues are resolved, I go to the next core as the Lord leads and repeat the process. If it's the Emotional Core, I usually see a lot of pain and emotional issues. If it's the Guardian, I sense resistance. The Lord must reveal how to make a way there. After all three cores have received the Lord, I then I pray for synchronization or joining them together in unity. Fragments in each core still usually need to be healed, but now each core has a foundation to build upon as each fragment is brought into healing and restoration.

Nadia Encountering Mother God?

I was praying for Nadia in the spirit realm. She was raised by a single mother without a father's influence in her life. She had also been molested in youth group and violently raped as an adult, resulting in well-founded and deep issues with men. As I was praying for her issues, I saw the Lord come to one of her fragments in the spirit realm as a woman. This was the only way she could accept His comfort. If He had come as a man, she would not have been comfortable receiving His hugs of love. Since He appeared to her as an older, motherly woman, Nadia could let the Lord hold her and then release her pain to Him. The fragment had an abortion in the past. Mother God held the fragment as she expelled the baby, and Father God was there to catch the baby and take the baby with Him to heaven.

Although I believed that God could appear to someone as a woman, this was a first for me. I was reminded that one of God's Names is El Shaddai, the many-breasted one. I saw the reality of El Shaddai as this fragment was healed, revealing the majesty of God to me in an even greater measure.

Chapter 22: Matt

Abby's Story—Complications and Human Spirits

I'd been praying with Abby for a while. We had already walked through the healing of quite a few of her fractured parts. Her process was more complex when compared with that of others, which made sense, considering how rough her childhood had been.

I was under the impression that we had gone deep and had healed many major issues when she began to share with me that she believed she had an alter personality living her life part of the time. Abby said this alter came out during difficult situations and lived on the surface of her being in a state of torment for maybe a day or two before she switched back into her normal "happy" personality. She was starting to believe that this was not just a different mood but a different personality taking over.

She had only recently been able to face this. She felt a lot of embarrassment about this "alter," as she called it, although it made perfect sense considering how much trauma she had endured at an early age.

We scheduled a session to pray for this part, but when the time came, I was led to reach out to another part first. I was shown a part who was like a controller behind the scenes, who made executive decisions for the system of parts, possibly deciding which ones were out when and similar matters. Diane and some others sometimes refer to this as a "gatekeeper part." I asked to talk to this one and was met quickly with a response.

This controller part was overwhelmed and exhausted, carrying much demonic oppression and pain. We walked her through freedom from many burdens, strongholds, and emotional issues before she met the Lord and was taken to a new location. She needed to receive the Lord as her Savior and to let Him empower her to function based on His ability, not merely her own. Jesus took her to a place that seemed to be a command center with futuristic technology where she could more effectively do her job within Abby.

Now that this controller part was in much better shape, I began to ask about the alter we originally planned to work with, and she had much to share on that subject.

She shared that this alter was held in captivity within a cavern by a "manager." Not only that, but she was like one of those Russian Matryoshka dolls, a doll within a doll within a doll, etc. Many parts were connected to this alter, descending deep into the cavern. These parts fit together as follows: angry, emotional, angry, emotional, and so forth throughout the whole structure.

These parts reportedly began at adulthood at the surface of the cavern and descended in age to infancy toward the back of the cavern where a string connected them all to a black abyss. I was receiving a mental picture of a treasure chest behind the abyss where some of Abby's gifts or possibly positive generational inheritances were hidden.

This information later turned out to be very helpful when beginning to pray with the parts in this cavern. Dealing with this manager first was key, and similar "managers" were found throughout the cavern, oppressing the various parts. I might have been led to detour and help the controller/gatekeeper part for the sake of getting this information beforehand.

Fractured Parts from Before Conception

Speaking of detours, right before Abby recognized that an alter had been living her life part-time, we took a significant step during the previous session that might have opened the door to this new level of self-awareness.

You might have heard of taking people back to the womb for inner healing. Many have found breakthrough by praying over their time in the womb, addressing generational strongholds and emotional woundedness from that period. As adults, we don't usually have conscious memories of our time in the womb, but we do tend to carry trauma from negative experiences at some level from that time. Diane and I have both found fractured parts from the womb and have found it very beneficial to heal them.

If you are interested in this subject, Restoration in Christ Ministries, headed by Diane Hawkins, has an excellent introduction and outline for praying over womb trauma as the Lord leads on their website.

I had been led to take a few clients back even further than the womb, to a time pre-conception when they were only spirits in a heavenly place. For some reason, people seem to carry generational strongholds and woundedness even from that time. I've walked people through the healing of fractured parts of their spirit originating back then.

Does Jeremiah 1 not tell us that the Lord knew us before He knit us together in our mother's womb? Could there not be a reality of life before conception?

Some might balk at the idea of spirits in heaven fracturing or carrying demonic oppression, but there seem to be many different levels and places in heaven. Some of these places are under human authority, so defilement can come in. Revelation 12:8 even speaks of Satan, the accuser, being in heaven and then cast out of heaven through spiritual warfare over earthly kingdoms and nations.

Most of those I've prayed with on this level have found that their spirit was heavily accused in a certain realm of heaven with the generational issues of the assigned family line already being used against them. I've seen this woundedness, as well as woundedness coming from the womb, set themes for lifetimes of struggle in specific areas.

I had just taken Abby back to her time in heaven before conception, and she found her spirit fractured and feeling very accused there. I walked fractured parts of her spirit through repenting for and renouncing the generational strongholds upon which accusations were based, repenting and renouncing on behalf of herself and all her ancestors. We resolved various strongholds of accusation and performance pressure, then allowed the Father to minister to her, nurturing and comforting her.

Along the way, I was leading Abby's spirit to renounce Satanism and child sacrifice from her generational line when another, later-formed fractured part began manifesting demons. We went on a rabbit trail to address this emergency and did deliverance on the manifesting part from heavy occult bondage, including issues from overt Satanic rituals done by ancestors. Counterfeit spirits persistently imitated the Lord to this part until we had her renounce them all, and she finally met the true Jesus. Jesus quickly took her to a place of rest. All that warfare had been pretty intense for her.

After this session, Abby started to recognize that she had an alter living her life part-time. The alter's "manager" turned out to be related to the Satanism she had just dealt with. This process might have been what uncovered the stronghold of the cavern. The enemy would have liked to keep it all hidden if possible.

Expect the Unexpected:
Introducing Disembodied Human Spirits

When we finally got around to reaching out to the alter itself, we found out that we first needed to deal with a "manager." Previously, we ran into hybrid demon-human parts holding various fragments of Abby in captivity. We found it necessary to separate the demonic from the human, to seek the human aspect's permission to remove the demonic, and then to heal up that part before we could access the other parts who it had been holding captive while joined to the enemy.

We had even run into something that first appeared as a demonic face on a ceiling that was trapping a part of Abby in a confined space. This demonic ceiling didn't respond to commands of authority in Christ to be removed, no matter how much the trapped part attempted to come out of agreement with it. Dealing with it as a hybrid demon-human part turned out to be effective, though, and the demonic ceiling turned into a little girl who was eager to be healed up. The formerly trapped part could be freed as a result.

I assumed this would be the same story, that a highly demonized or hybrid demon-human part would be the manager and that it would be necessary to minister to it first before the ones it was oppressing. However, I was led to pray differently.

The first clue that this was not the usual situation was that I was led to put the manager in prison and to ignore him while working with the alter. I questioned what I was sensing in prayer, not wanting to put a part in prison when it could just be delivered and healed. It is typically better to treat parts more gently when working with them instead of immediately putting them in prison. Earning their trust is an important key to healing.

I prayed that the manager would be completely restrained and unable to cause any problems, and I began reaching out to the alter of which Abby had become aware. Just as the gatekeeper had said, there was both an angry part and an emotional part to this alter, and they each carried tremendous burdens.

Both parts were covered in occult paraphernalia and needed to be walked through much generational renunciation from issues such as divination, necromancy, Satanism, astrology, secret societies, séances, new age and psychic practices, false religions, blood covenants with demons, human and animal sacrifices, etc. We faced spiritual resistance along the way as they broke agreement with the occult pacts their ancestors had made.

We also took some extra time to listen to these parts tell their stories about how much anger and pain they carried and about how they functioned in Abby's life. They shared how "Happy Abby" went around acting as if nothing were wrong while these two carried intense anger and pain over everything Abby seemed to let roll off her back as if she were the perfect, un-offendable Christian. On the surface, she seemed to always walk in peace, joy, and forgiveness, regardless of anything anybody did to her, but under the surface, these parts were suffering grievously.

The parts were not happy that they had to carry all the pain and hatred buried underneath. They didn't like the fact that Abby wasn't listening to them, helping them deal with their burdens, or responding with appropriate boundaries toward people to stop them from being hurt further. Abby needed to apologize to these parts and to reconcile with them before they would find full healing. She needed to commit to learning new ways of managing emotions and life situations.

These two were fused together into one part but not yet integrated into Abby. They seemed to need to be joined by the other parts from the cavern before integration would take place.

We went back to check on the bound manager, thinking this was probably another part needing help. He turned out to be an older man who had been bound in chains and stuck to a wall. He was raging and rebellious.

I bound up all his demons and restrained them from manipulating or controlling him, asking him if he wanted freedom from them. He said no. I asked him why he didn't want freedom from these controlling and tormenting demons, and he answered that it was because they gave him power. I replied that they sure weren't giving him much power while he was chained up on that wall.

It was becoming pretty clear that he was not a part of Abby but was something else I had run into from time to time over the years—a disembodied human spirit who was lost after death. In this case, he was trapped by the enemy, used for evil purposes. I've found that the Lord will redeem these "lost sheep" in the afterlife just as surely as He is willing to redeem any other person from their sins. Why wouldn't He?

Contrary to what we are probably used to hearing from modern preachers, I've found that the blood of Jesus does not stop being effective for people after their physical death. I'll explain more about that a little bit later.

I shared that the Lord had a better destiny for this man in heaven, that he didn't have to do this job anymore, that the Lord had already carried all his sins on the cross and so forgiveness and redemption, even now, wasn't any problem.

His immediate answer was that he didn't care, but after a bit, he began to realize that he was chained up, stuck to the wall with nowhere to go, and had no other choices. He decided then that he did want to be delivered. I commanded the demons to be removed from him and then led him in renouncing all sorts of occult activities before removing more demons.

When I asked him if he had any more evil spirits that he needed to come out of agreement with before meeting Jesus, he confessed that he had been a Satanist during his life who had made an agreement with Death. He was put on assignment in the afterlife to torment these parts of Abby, and he began to share how he operated. He kept these pain-filled parts of her locked up in the cavern until the worst times possible and would force them to come to the surface of her life just when it would cause the most turmoil.

He broke his agreements with Satanism and Death, repenting from his assignment to torment Abby. Now that the major oppression was lifted from him, his deeper emotions began to surface. He was weeping for his sons, worried that if he went to heaven, his boys would be left behind. He wanted to find his sons first.

I told him that I didn't know what was going on with his sons or if we could help them anytime soon but that Jesus could show him. He agreed to that. Jesus came to minister to him upon invitation and began showing him a passageway into heaven. He didn't want to go there until he could bring his lost sons with him who had been caught up in similar activities.

This man's sons were buried in Abby as well. I saw them wrapped up in something similar to cellophane wrapping, and I asked them if they wanted to be free from the demonic control. I stated that all they had to do was say yes in their hearts even though they couldn't speak or move physically. I commanded them to be freed, assuming that they were probably saying yes when faced with the alternative.

They were freed and brought to their father as he stood with Jesus. We had a sense that they all followed Jesus into heaven, and that was the last we heard from them as we worked through the rest of the cavern.

I don't claim to be an expert at dealing with these lost disembodied spirits, but I have worked with them a number of times and have seen positive results in people's lives. Folks seem to be delivered from the demonic oppression, emotional issues, and even physical ailments that these lost human spirits carried while living inside them.

Some of these spirits seem to be on assignment from the enemy after making an agreement with Death as this Satanist had. Some of them seem to be passed down their family line to influence and contaminate their own descendants, possibly due to generational occult bondage, controlling family ties, or both. These might be what Scripture refers to as familiar spirits, which in the original language is more like familial spirits.

Other disembodied human spirits seem to literally be lost with no evil agenda other than to have an emotional need met. Some seem to just want someone to commiserate with, so they find a person carrying similar pains and problems as themselves and jump into them when they see an open door. Others seem to be offended at God and unwilling to move into eternity. They seem to end up wandering around, kind of hitchhiking from person to person.

Many people in ministry have run into these spirits and have learned to minister to them and to move them into eternity, although many disagree vastly about the belief systems involved.

Arthur Burk has recorded three long and in-depth series of messages about this subject that have been widely influential, but his take is a bit different than mine. He isn't the only one involved in this type of ministry but is one of the few who have publicly taught about it. Diane and I are compiling testimonies of our work in this realm and plan to publish a book of detailed accounts. We will go into much more depth there.

I've noticed some healing and deliverance ministers who have come up with an entirely different interpretation after running into these people living inside their clients who are clearly not a part of the client, clearly human rather than demon, and who seem to have lived in previous generations. These ministers claim that these are "generational fragments" or "generational alters," literally fractured parts of one's ancestors who have been passed down the line. They believe that the Lord comes and heals these "parts," taking them out of the person and into heaven rather than integrating them into the client.

I have found that ministering to disembodied spirits is very much like ministering to fractured parts. They are human after all, and many of the same principles will apply. I've also found that some folks do have fractured parts of other people living within them due to soul ties, which can be ministered to just like any other part before being sent back to the person from whom they originally came. Sometimes, these even play aggressive and tormenting roles in a person's system if the relationship they had with that person was abusive or controlling.

Further complicating matters, one's parts can sometimes be disguised as another person. They might even be disguised as another person by the enemy and used to cause trouble, possibly due to how the younger parts respond to the disguise. As they are delivered, their disguise comes off, and we find out whose parts they really are. Not everything in this realm is simple and easy to discern at first glance.

The final take on this topic is subject to the discernment and interpretation of the people praying. Regardless of exactly what we think these spirits or parts are, they can be delivered, healed up by the Lord, and moved on to their intended destination in very similar ways.

Even so, my experience and the experience of those I trust is that we are often dealing with the disembodied spirits of those who have passed on but who haven't yet made it to their God-given destiny in heaven.

I've run into numerous of these who claimed that they were in league with the enemy, made agreements with Death, and were functioning in the afterlife according to his agenda. After they were met with superior power and offered a way out, they have turned to the Lord and moved on with Him, resulting in a positive difference in the lives of their previous hosts.

Many other scenarios have played out with human spirits telling different stories of their backgrounds before moving out of their host and moving on with the Lord. I see no reason to re-interpret any of this for the sake of lining up with a theology based in fear and condemnation.

I've usually tried to reach out to these human spirits to offer them healing and an encounter with Jesus to help meet their needs. Sometimes, that is all that is necessary, but at other times, deliverance is needed first. You might need to realize that these spirits aren't lost in the afterlife because they are in a wonderful condition and delighted at the idea of receiving Jesus as their Lord and Savior. They often have a history of occultism or deep wounds, of resistance to the Gospel and the true Light even if they aren't overtly in league with evil.

I typically start just as I do with fractured parts, by binding up and restraining anything demonic that is manipulating or controlling them. I offer them freedom from the demons and from any trap in which they might be locked up. Just as with fractured parts, these human spirits will usually jump at the opportunity for freedom.

Evicting any controlling demonization seems to help them and to put me on their good side.

I try to discern and listen to them, seeing if they want to share their story or share anything from their heart. I offer them healing for their hurts and try to recognize where the Lord could meet their needs. They are usually in pretty bad shape and up for at least trying out an encounter with Jesus after I explain how He is the one who gave me authority to heal and deliver them from various issues. I often explain that He is all love and is nothing like the condemning, mean "Jesus" of religion.

If they accept my offer to meet with Jesus, I usually walk them through some generational renunciation, just as with parts, to make sure they meet the real Jesus. I have them examine whoever shows up to make sure that this is indeed the real Jesus, evicting any impostors one by one if needed.

Once the real Jesus shows up, it's pretty much over. He quickly melts their hearts and resolves any objections. He loves them, heals them up further, and leads them into glory.

If the human spirits are very obstinate, such as those committed to an enemy agenda, I might need to remove them forcibly. At times, I've found it effective to simply command them to go; other times, that hasn't seemed to work. Some people who work in this area have reported calling on angels with chains to drag the most rebellious human spirits away to a place of confinement.

In the worst cases, I've needed to pull out the head human spirit from the person by force along with all his underlings. The worst ones seem to have groups arranged in a hierarchy underneath them and under the enemy, in other words, a military unit. By faith, I drag them all into the court of heaven to receive judgment. I usually do this with a group so that I have a team working with me and don't miss any important discernment.

I've found that the moment right before starting the trial, when they can see the judge and all the heavenly beings present to decide their fate, is a perfect time to offer them another chance to repent. I will explain what is about to happen, that they will never be allowed back to torment their old host, but they will be given a chance to move on to heaven if they repent. If they don't, they will be sent to some other place of confinement that I can't promise will be any fun.

I've found that even the worst and most stubborn human spirits have laid down their agreements with Death and the occult as they see judgment about to be passed against them. At this point, I will walk them through deliverance and healing just as with fractured parts, then start their case when they are ready. They might ask questions or request help at any time, and heaven is glad to work with them as they do so.

As judgment is passed, the human spirits are given a choice to stand on one side of the courtroom or the other based on the fate they agree to. So far, almost all of them have seemed to move into glory at the end. I think I can confidently say that these examples have been some of the worst demonically loyal offenders of all human spirits. As such, I'd say that most of these ones moving on to heaven is a pretty good outcome.

Is This Heresy?

Many who have grown up in the church become uncomfortable if you start talking about Satanists or other offenders being redeemed in the afterlife. They might feel that God's justice requires such people to be punished indefinitely due to the sins they committed on earth.

Many have only been exposed to one theology about the afterlife, which is that people leave their bodies and are immediately sent to heaven or hell forever. However, other views are at least as well supported scripturally, and we aren't yet in the afterlife, so we are unable to fully test whether our theories are correct. Many have been told that all views other than that of their group are simply unbiblical and heretical.

I was also influenced by this popular view found in many modern churches that you die and that there are "no second chances," so you immediately go to heaven or hell forever. Scripture was interpreted this way for me by preachers who seemed to know what they were talking about, and I became conditioned to look at any other views with extreme suspicion.

When a friend became convinced that all souls would eventually be redeemed in the afterlife and that the spiritual realms of darkness and torment are not what we previously thought in our more common theology as "hell," I was at first concerned for her. Was she sliding off into total heresy, possibly falling away from her salvation? Today, that reaction seems comical to me, and I'm not proud to admit I had it. I now view that as no different than freaking out over someone's different view of the "end times," as if such a highly speculative and relatively obscure subject were absolutely essential to our faith.

I listened to my friend and began to research the arguments she used to support her new view of what Scripture had to say about the afterlife. The more I examined the arguments between the proponents of eternal torment, annihilationism, and universal reconciliation, the more I began to realize that the Bible wasn't nearly as cut and dry on the subject as popular preachers had made it sound. I found very logical points made about key Greek and Hebrew words and the context of various passages that appeared to support a position I had written off as dangerous and unbiblical.

The strong biblical arguments for multiple positions cast doubt on the claim that eternal torture is the only possibility. I couldn't dogmatically hold to such a harsh position without rock-solid evidence for it in the Bible, and I was beginning to consider that maybe there wasn't any. I am no Hebrew or Greek scholar, although we do live in the information age with easy-to-use original language tools at our fingertips that allow us to research material only "experts" could previously access. As someone new to this debate, I wasn't going to jump to conclusions about these matters without taking a lot more time to examine them.

I asked the Lord to show me the truth about whether He was going to let those who pass on as unbelievers be freed from the bad place at some point during the afterlife. He seemed to show me that yes, indeed, He was going to rescue them. I believe that He also showed me to use discretion about who I talked to about the subject at the time. I was about to join a ministry school that was not at all open to this perspective, and I didn't need to add yet another controversial idea to those I was already sharing to hinder my chances of people coming to know me before reacting in fear over some speculative doctrine.

I put the issue of what exactly "hell" was and how long people are going to be there on the shelf as a minor issue in the larger picture of my beliefs. I was more focused on growing in my relationship with God and in becoming more effective at reaching and helping people through the work of the Spirit. I wanted to see the world reached and transformed, regardless of exactly how many "ages of the ages" people will be trapped by the enemy in the afterlife before the Lord is able to rescue them. (This phrase, "ages of the ages," is possibly a better translation of a phrase in Revelation 14:11 that is hotly debated among proponents of eternal torment and universal reconciliation.)

As I became less involved with ministry groups that might have become upset and ostracized me if I had taken a strong, public position against their afterlife theology and, as I looked at the issue empathetically from the perspective of a hurting person who was just trying to figure out whether the Christian God was good or whether the message of Jesus made any sense, I again examined the subject of the afterlife.

I had encounters and conversations with the Lord and was shown more on the subject. I did more research into various passages of Scripture in question. I found the materials of Richard Murray to be especially helpful in scripturally demonstrating a positive image of God and an ultimately loving theology of the afterlife. He has a free book, *The Question of Hell*, which is especially scholarly and informative, on his website, www.thegoodnessofgod.com.

When I began to run into lost human spirits while praying with people for healing and when I found out that many strong believers and leaders in the Body of Christ had been encountering the same thing, this subject took a whole new, more practical direction for me. Not only was I seeing it as a matter of how good and loving we viewed and presented God to be, but this was directly related to whether or not suffering people would be free in this life and in the next.

This journey spanned over a decade, and I have come to some firm conclusions. At the same time, I realize that not everyone is going to take a decade to make their own decisions about this. I run into plenty of people who intuitively feel that they recognize the truth and can accept it all immediately.

I'm going to share a few thoughts on Scripture and church history below that I hope might call into question any rigid views out there that eternal torment is the only honest way to interpret the Bible. I don't expect everyone to immediately agree with all my views, but I aim to at least start you thinking for yourself about it.

In pushing the idea that there is only one obvious way to interpret the Bible when it comes to the afterlife, many Christians are quick to cite a few isolated verses that they consider to support a doctrine that once somebody dies, their fate is sealed with no "second chances." They believe that throwing out a few of these passages settles the matter, making it clear that human spirits can't possibly be wandering around among people in this world.

2 Corinthians 5:8 is one such verse, "to be absent from the body and to be at home with the Lord," which many people use to make a very rigid theology about the afterlife. They insist that because this verse says, "absent from the body and to be at home with the Lord," you immediately translate into heaven or hell after you die with no middle ground. What they don't seem to realize is that Paul was talking about himself and his ministry team here, not unbelievers.

Hebrews 9:27 is another such verse, "And inasmuch as it is appointed for men to die once and after this comes judgment." As an isolated verse, this might seem to support the idea that after you die, your chances are up. In context, though, this speaks about the death of Jesus Christ for all mankind so that none of us have to die or to face a punitive judgment for our sins. In context, the verse is saying the exact opposite of what it appears to say in isolation.

Who appointed man to die? I don't think God is appointing man to die, but Satan is appointing death for us. 1 Corinthians 15:26 tells us that death is an enemy of God, so how is it that this enemy supposedly switched sides for one verse?

If there are no "second chances," if God has put a firm rule in place that after you die, your time is up and you must face your final judgment, why did Jesus go around raising people from the dead, breaking His Father's rules? Why did He send His disciples out to raise the dead and then command them to teach all nations to do everything that He had them doing? Did Jesus institute a massive rebellion against His Father's rule that people die once and then face their final judgment?

What exactly is the judgment spoken of in this verse? Do you realize that this could be something positive for the person being judged? Why did David cry out for the Lord to judge him over and over throughout the Psalms? I believe that God's judgment is a blessing, a purification process, that leads to our betterment.

The Greek word translated "punishment" in Scripture, as in "depart from me into aionios punishment," means beneficial correction. It is the word "kolasis." According to Aristotle, the ancient world's foremost authority on Greek word meanings, this means correction that benefits the one being corrected as opposed to another Greek word, "timoria," meaning punishment/correction as revenge (Strong).

Jesus only ever used "kolasis." "Timoria" is never found in in direct relation to the Father's actions (it is never found in His heart), but is used twice to describe Saul's persecution of Christians before he became Paul. It is also used once in Hebrews 10 as a speculation of what people who trample the blood of Jesus could be "thought worthy of."

The words translated "eternal" in Scripture are also key to further understanding additional opportunities for salvation in the afterlife. "Aion" and its variations, "aionios" and "aionion," are often translated as "eternal," yet they don't speak of a duration of time in classical Greek usage apart from Platonic philosophy where they were used as inseparable from an "eternal" deity. They more accurately refer to a source of something, not its duration. In the New Testament, the same words are typically translated as "this age," "the ages," "the world," and "eternal," among a few other options. The option chosen is entirely up to the discretion of the translator (Hanson).

Sadly, much has been lost in translation when it comes to passages referencing the afterlife. Biased translators have often written their own doctrines based in fear and condemnation into the English versions of Scripture. A small amount of research easily proves this.

As a little bread crumb to start you on this path, the word most often translated as "hell" does not actually mean hell as we understand it. Instead, this word, "Gehenna," was a physical location in Israel (Strong). It was likely in a bad area of town, but I'm sure that it wasn't literally "hell." It was a garbage dump used as an allegory of life outside of God's Kingdom.

The passage that references the lake of fire pictured in the book of Revelation also states that the people in this "lake of fire" are "in the presence of the Lamb" at the same time! Revelation speaks of dragons flying through space doing battle with a woman standing on the moon, prophets with flamethrowers in their mouths, stars falling to the earth and killing some of the people on it, etc. Nearly all Bible scholars agree that these are symbolic images, which might well be the case with the lake of fire. This might refer to the baptism in the Holy Spirit and fire that John the Baptist spoke of when he declared that the Messiah would "thoroughly purge his threshing floor."

Scripture uses enough metaphorical language when referring to these subjects so that even the greatest scholars, who lived nearest to the time of the original writings, vastly disagree. The leading bishops of the early church held and taught radically different beliefs from each other about the fate of unbelievers in the afterlife.

In the third century, the majority view and the view of the most influential bishop, Origen of Alexandria, was universal reconciliation for all of mankind. He taught that "the wise fire of God" would purify the souls of unbelievers unto salvation in the afterlife. This was based on an understanding of the original Scriptures in his native Greek tongue, and the majority of leading bishops of his day agreed with him (Murray 9-10).

A few bishops taught annihilationism, the belief that unbelievers would completely "perish" into nonexistence in the afterlife. Eternal torment was a minority view taught by the Bishop of Rome, whose successors gained influence in later centuries. Later, during the leadership of Augustine in the fourth century, who was highly influenced by Neo-Platonic philosophy and dependent on a translation into his Latin tongue after losing track of the Greek Scriptures, the view of eternal torment became a more mainstream doctrine due to the influence of his teaching (Murray 13).

Still, as late as the eighth century, men like Gregory of Nyssa, who had the final say on the formation of the Nicene Creed, were firm, public believers in universal reconciliation (Murray 11).

Today, though, many will act as if eternal torment is the only possible interpretation of what Scripture says about the afterlife, as if you are just throwing the Bible away if you disagree with their theology. They gloss over Ephesians 1:10, which declares that "all things will be 'summed up' (brought together as one) in Christ." If all things will be brought together as one in Christ, this begs the question of who will be separated from Him forever.

Colossians 1:20 further declares that God intends on reconciling "all things to himself." Given all eternity, is He not able to accomplish what He intends? Romans 5:18-19 states, "So then as through one transgression there resulted condemnation to all men, even so through one act of righteousness there resulted justification of life to all men. For as through the one man's disobedience the many were made sinners, even so through the obedience of the One the many will be made righteous" Similar verses are typically glossed over all throughout the Bible, appearing to paint a much more hopeful future for all of mankind than we might have previously heard.

Many will call you a "universalist" if you believe that God will eventually reach all people, but this view differs greatly from Unitarian Universalism, which believes that all religions lead to the same god and that Jesus is not necessary for salvation. I believe that Jesus is the only way but that he will eventually have His way and will reach, rescue, and heal even the most bound and bruised captives of the enemy.

Going Deep into the Cavern

I intended to heal another layer of this "Matryoshka doll" making up the "alter" trapped in the cavern. As we prayed at the beginning of our next session, I was shown an image of a box with black smoke pouring out if it. I was led to pray that the black smoke would be stuffed back into the box.

I had a sense of being led to go after the bottom depths of the cavern where the parts that were the ages of infants would be, but Abby was shown an eight-year-old part. I deferred to what she was sensing, and it turned out that this eight-year-old had the box of black smoke. The purpose of the smoke was to maintain denial, to hide things that the parts in the cavern didn't want to see about themselves.

I questioned this girl about her issues, and we removed some surface-level hurts. However, she clearly wasn't willing to talk about deeper problems. I backed off for the moment and walked her through some generational renunciations for every occult issue I could list, expecting that this girl was just as oppressed by generational witchcraft as the parts on the surface of the cavern were.

An even younger girl appeared in a black dress and black cape, spinning circles with a sense of great eeriness. As the older girl finished the occult renunciations, the younger one stopped spinning, which seemed positive.

The older girl wanted her box of black smoke back, but I told her that it was only keeping her in torment and keeping her from being healed. I shared that truth wasn't what she thought. It wasn't something to be afraid of or something that merely exposes us and condemns us. Real truth exposes how loved we are and exposes our higher purpose. It heals us so that we don't need to hide anymore.

She was afraid to share her deeper hurts, so I sought her permission to have the fear removed, and after I commanded it to go, she became free and willing to share. She was carrying tremendous self-loathing issues. I offered to put up a movie from heaven in front of her to show her what God had to say to her. She agreed to watch it.

As soon as I declared by faith that the movie was playing, a demon grabbed her and started pulling her away from it. She had to come out of agreement with that demon on behalf of herself and her ancestors so that she could finish watching the message. She was shown all sorts of wonderful things about who she was and quickly agreed that all her shame and self-hatred should be removed along with the lies she had believed about her identity. We accomplished this through a command of faith.

I shared with her that the movie had shown her the real truth and that the black smoke was hiding the good things from her. She agreed to have the box of smoke fully removed. When it left, Abby's mental clarity and spiritual perception increased noticeably. The eight-year-old shared about deep rejection issues and became willing to receive healing for them as well.

The younger girl who Abby had seen spinning in a black cape earlier was identified as a part within the eight-year-old part. The purpose of the spinning was to spread occult influence throughout the cavern.

This younger one didn't want to renounce the occult because she saw it as her identity. I told her that, just as the older one thought her identity was in her shame, her faults, and in all the rejection she had suffered, that wasn't who she truly was, so she wasn't who she thought she was. She wasn't truly evil.

I again used the same technique with the younger girl; I offered to put up a movie to show her what the Lord had to say about who she was. She accepted. Watching the movie, she became willing to renounce all the occult and demonic activities she had clung to so tightly before.

The older one was very curious, asking about how deep the cavern went, how tall she was, etc. I asked if we could invite Jesus to answer her questions. She agreed to that. Our first attempt at inviting Jesus brought a man who mostly looked good but who had deception in his eyes. I had the part renounce deception and various issues surrounding deception on behalf of herself and her ancestors, commanding all of that to go. That man instantly disappeared.

Our next invitation brought the true Jesus with love in His eyes. Jesus began to answer the many questions of both parts in ways that helped them with their deepest issues. The younger one thought she was always going to be small and limited. When she asked Jesus how tall she was going to be, He showed her that she could be as tall as she wanted. He took her up to her seat in heavenly places and said, "You can even be this tall! You can be above everything and able to see everything!"

They asked Jesus what love was. He held them, telling them that it was found in rest, that they didn't have to do anything, that nothing was expected, and that He had no agenda but to love them as they were. As I asked what Jesus wanted to do next, He put love into their hearts so that they could feel it. He did several more things to minister to deep issues.

Jesus exchanged the younger girl's black dress for a white one and said, "Try twirling in that!" This spread a positive influence instead of an evil one as she spun around. He took them outside the cavern to a "secret place," which was something they had always wanted— to be included among friends and told where all the coolest and most secret places were in the woods around their neighborhood.

Jesus shared that He wanted to fuse the two girls together in this place and then fuse them with the other one who had already been rescued from the cavern. The younger girl needed to be delivered from fear before she was ready for this, but they did go through with it.

The newly fused part, now in heaven, received a crown from Jesus along with ministry to her mind, unlocking hidden memories and understanding. She became aware of more about the younger parts in the cavern. The youngest was revealed as a part of her as a spirit from even before conception, which was trapped in an evil eye.

We asked Jesus to remove her from the eye and to minister to her, and He did so. He immediately took her out of the cavern and brought her to heaven with the recently fused part, beginning to minister to her needs. He walked her through renouncing the same generational occult issues the others had.

While Jesus was ministering to the little part of the spirit, somebody else was seen hiding nearby, a young girl who intended to nab the rescued part of the spirit to put it back inside the evil eye. Abby and I were laughing about the fact that someone thought they could spy on Jesus and take back the part from Him. This little spy girl was identified as another disembodied human spirit with an assignment from the enemy.

I was going to bind and restrain the demonic and then move forward as I often do with these human spirits, but I stopped myself and said, "I'd rather just see how Jesus handles it."

Jesus asked the spirit, "What are you doing here?"

She answered, "I have an assignment to bring her back."

Jesus replied, "Is that something you want to do, or is it just something somebody else wants you to do?" She said that she was afraid of punishment if she didn't do it. Jesus asked, "Who told you to do this?" She pointed to a little bug in her ear, a demon who was bossing her around.

Jesus said that he could get rid of that bug so that she didn't have to listen to it or do what it said anymore. She was happy to let Him do that, tired of having to obey it all the time. He shared that He could be her Savior and take her to heaven so that she wouldn't need to go back to the cavern, and she gladly agreed.

She wanted to help with the healing process. She shared that she had been put in charge of three more young parts besides the preconception spirit: an infant, a two-year-old, and a three-year-old. The enemy had assigned her to be like an older sister to all these parts, watching over them and keeping them in bondage.

She shared that other, older parts were also in the cavern, but she wasn't in charge of them. Older human spirits oversaw those. We were learning that, besides the Satanist we had first encountered, other guards were apparently over various parts in the cavern according to age.

The newly converted girl was especially scared of one human spirit and didn't even like talking about him.

I couldn't resist asking Jesus if we could bait the scary one to challenge him, asking him to reassure the little human spirit that she would be okay. He had the little one stand behind his leg. The spirit she feared was already on his way, marching up to Jesus.

He was a large and rough man who got right up in Jesus' face, yelling, "What do you think you're doing here? You're messing up everything!" Jesus simply touched him on the nose, and he fell unconscious. Abby and I were laughing and having so much fun with this!

Jesus said that He was just going to remove that one so that he wouldn't have any influence in the cavern anymore. He wasn't going to do anything further with him at the moment.

Another disembodied spirit, a sensual woman who was second in command under the scary guy, was also present. She was like a madam while the scary guy acted like a pimp. Her job seemed to be to infect the parts in the cavern with sexual addiction.

She seemed to be hiding. By faith, I grabbed her and pulled her over to where Jesus was, and she suddenly appeared on the ground before Him. She was joined to the demonic, full of shame, and stark naked. Jesus put a blanket over her body and sought her permission to evict the demons, and she quickly agreed. He showed her who she used to be before she became so corrupted and who He intended her to be. He began to heal her of her immorality and wounds.

Jesus continued ministering to the madam as well as to the younger girl who had first come to spy, showing them how He saw them in His eyes of love and purpose, helping them to receive further healing.

It was getting late, and we asked Jesus if we needed to stay involved or if He would continue ministering to these spirits without us, as well as to the part of Abby's spirit taken from the evil eye. He seemed to confirm that He would continue whether we were there or not, and we called it a night.

Interestingly, at the beginning of the session, I was shown to pray over the black box and then shown to minister to the youngest part at the very back of the cavern, but Abby was shown the eight-year-old who owned the black box. Ministering to the eight-year-old not only finished resolving the issue with the box but led to Jesus rescuing the very youngest part at the back of the cavern.

More than once, I've found that what I'm shown at the beginning of a session will truly play out, yet differently than I expected when I received it.

In the next session, we reached out to a fourteen-year-old part in the cavern. She needed some bondages broken so that she could wake up from a deep sleep and some additional issues resolved so that she could think clearly. A spirit was pinching a nerve in her brain, and she needed to come out of agreement with this as well as deal with other oppressions.

She benefitted from the standard occult renunciations that other parts in this cavern had done along with more personalized prayers. We identified and healed emotional issues. A crow nested above her head, picking at her brain, making a nest of memories it had removed from her. The crow needed to be removed, and the memories reclaimed.

A being was behind her who claimed to be giving her peace but who was only putting her to sleep, and we had to remove it. An intimidating panther was seen crouched and ready to attack. When I had her break agreement with it, instead of leaving, it began to attack her. I could bind it up and stop it from doing harm, but in this case, she needed to discern and renounce a specific generational sin rather than just renouncing the panther itself.

Two little gingerbread men were even dancing at her feet, seeming just to entertain her, but these were identified as bad spirits as was nearly everything else in this cavern. They were removed as well.

Breaking agreement with the spirit of Death was especially beneficial for this part.

When we invited Jesus to come, an empty-eyed, religious "Jesus" showed up, and the girl quickly broke agreement with him. Next, the real Jesus walked in, and He put her reclaimed memories in water to bring them back to life. She became aware of old emotions long repressed. He also took her out of the cavern to be cleansed in a pool of water in the garden of Abby's heart.

This part came from a time in Abby's life when many tragedies had struck her family, when she had stuffed all the pain into fractured parts, and hadn't even mourned the death of close loved ones. She had become gothic and had taken on a dark identity, settling into deep depression for a period.

Jesus shared with her that she was not a person of darkness and depression as she thought but that she was a person of great compassion, which was why her emotions were so sensitive. The pain buried in her heart was so strong that she needed to be put to sleep for it to be removed so that the process was not too overwhelming.

Her memories and deep emotions were surfacing even more now that some of the pain was gone, and I asked if she would like the rest of the anger, shame, and pain removed from them. She responded negatively because she "hadn't even processed them yet." I had her ask Jesus if He wanted her to process her memories with the pain still intact or without it, and He replied that He wanted to take away the pain first. She let Him remove it.

He took her to meet with the other, fused part who was now a conglomeration of all others taken from the cavern so far. He let her rest there.

Next, we found a child part terrorized by evil spirits and nightmares. She needed the typical occult renunciations followed by identification and removal of bad spirits. A human boy was also there with a sheet with holes draped over him in a corny attempt at being scary.

He turned out to a spirit or fragment of a boy that this young girl had liked in elementary school, and ties needed to be broken with him before he could be removed and sent back to his original core person.

This young girl was finally brought to the garden to see the other parts.

Next, we ministered to an adult part toward the surface of the cavern who was carrying a lot of disillusionment and pain about family relationships. In addition to the usual occult renunciations, her heart needed to be healed from deep pain and shame.

A key was revealed around her neck, and Abby glimpsed a high-tech command center where she seemed to belong, though everything in it was broken down. A human spirit was identified as watching over her to keep her in bondage within the cavern, and I simply bound and restrained him before inviting Jesus to come minister to her.

Jesus took her to a new location to rest. She seemed to be a functional/task-oriented part of Abby, and the command center seemed to have something to do with exercising authority over the enemy.

In our next session, we got in touch with this older part again and let Jesus take her to the command center. This part of her heart seemed to be on lockdown with the entrance guarded by two big men—human spirits.

One of the men fled at the sight of Jesus, but the other stood firm, being commanded by a small being nearby to hold his ground. Jesus picked up the small being and blew on it, causing it to be revealed as a part of Abby. This part was adamant that it wasn't going to let anyone into this area of her heart.

Jesus explained that He wasn't going in there to hurt her like others had but was going in to make things better. He sought her permission to remove the demonic and the hurts, and she became willing to let Him into the room. At this point, the remaining human spirit ran off as well.

The little part had a small key that matched the larger key the older part held around her neck, and they both fit into keyholes on the doorway to this room. Entering, Jesus simply waved His hand and set everything right, fixing all the broken electronics.

However, a dark silhouette of a part that seemed to be the sleeping spirit of a fractured part rather than the whole part itself was still in this room. Jesus revealed that the rest of the part had been taken into captivity, and He reclaimed it from a place of torment where it had been captured during a demonic visitation at a young age.

Jesus healed the part He had just reclaimed from captivity, joined it together with the silhouette/spirit, and finished healing up the other two parts who had brought keys to the room.

They all began feasting and celebrating in this room of Abby's heart, affirming that this place in her that had been long shut down was good and was a place of intimacy with God rather than a place to fear.

Finally, Jesus washed, nourished, and clothed these parts in white before integrating them. Abby found her attitudes toward her family members changing significantly for the better after this experience.

This was neither the end of Abby's process nor even the end of her process working through this cavern, but this might be enough to provide you with some insights. You might see how human spirits can be involved in the oppression of fractured parts, especially when heavy occult bondage is in the generational line. Notice how easy and even fun it can be for the Lord to resolve this.

Abby is an example of someone with a rough childhood. Even so, most people wouldn't expect her to be dealing with such complex issues. Her relationship with God was strong, and her life seemed stable. She had never personally been involved in Satanism, heavy occult activity, or been ritually abused.

This begs the question of how her parts were literally oppressed by the spirit of a Satanist implanted within her, and carrying extensive bondage to the occult without her personal involvement. It was all generational. Her ancestors had opened the doors, and those spirits had travelled down the line to oppress their descendants, including Abby.

You might see signs of such open doors from previous generations. I've noticed that mental illness tends to run in these families. These people do tend to have hard childhoods due to family brokenness and dysfunction, but their woundedness seems to go far beyond the expected results of that. They seem to have many demonic encounters from a young age, especially at night.

They might suffer with demonic oppression that traditional deliverance ministry never resolves because the complex system of fractured parts is giving footholds to the various spirits and because many of the "demons" are not actually demons. Parts have taken on the role of playing demons or have become hybridized with demons. Entire organized groups of human spirits are working with the enemy to terrorize and control the parts. In some cases, occultists living today might continue to have assignments to watch over these people and further oppress them through open doors among their parts.

You can get to the bottom of all of this and resolve it, but it will usually be a long journey, not a quick prayer session or two. The reason it takes a long time is not because it is any harder for God but because God won't force healing on all the unreached, fractured parts or upon people who are using their free will to resist Him. Even though these people and their parts often want healing and might even be crying out to God for it, He won't force it on them when they haven't let go of their agreements with the enemy.

Overt agreements with demons must be renounced, and permission must be given for the Lord to remove hatred, resentment, and shame. Overt sins must be renounced and handed over by every part for the Lord to completely remove them. These footholds of the enemy must be actively resolved. We aren't dealing with evil people, but the enemy has deceived them into giving place to complex strongholds that keep out the Lord and keep in the demons.

If God ignored all this and instantly brought complete healing, He would have to renege on the gift of free will and personal authority He has given us. He wants to heal us more than we could ever want to be healed, but He simply will not take our freedom away to do it. This is why the system of internal woundedness must be worked through over time. The person and their parts must uncover and choose to surrender these areas which have been handed over to darkness.

Many receive quick healing of surface-level issues, such as a disease condition or a demon, but I'm talking about something different here: resolving deep and complex strongholds. In many instances, resolving these deeper and more complex wounds will lead to healing of surface issues rooted in those areas as well. I've seen people attain physical healing and deliverance in this way from issues that could never seem to be resolved otherwise, no matter who prayed for them.

Chapter 23: Matt

Tips for Ministering to Others

As you begin to put all of this into practice for yourself, you'll undoubtedly run into others who need help. We encourage you to step out and work with those you come across.

In this process of freedom, one of the unfortunate things we come across is methods that not only don't work but that usher in even greater bondage than before. This realm of integrating the various parts of our souls and spirits is confusing enough without muddying the waters further, so it seems prudent to discuss how to walk out this process with wisdom and discernment.

Start out Slowly

Begin your ministry to parts with finding healing for yourself, possibly with the help of someone experienced. Then, begin ministering to friends and simple, easier cases. Gain some experience before moving on to working with more severe woundedness.

If you want to work with people's deep hurts, you must first be willing to open up your own areas of brokenness and to walk through healing yourself. This isn't because you need to have it all together or be totally healed to help someone else (you don't) but because you need to be willing to subject yourself to the same level of scrutiny to which you are subjecting others.

Many people seem to want to minister but "don't have time" to receive ministry. I'm suspicious of these people's motives for ministering. Why would they want you to be vulnerable before them if they are afraid of opening up themselves? This doesn't seem as if they are loving people so much as they are loving being in a position of power over people.

Also, receiving healing gives you a more practical kind of knowledge. You begin to understand it from the inside, from the seat of the person receiving help. It becomes real to you rather than only a theory.

In addition, we become better at ministering to others in these areas with practice. If you start with the easy cases among people with whom you already have trusting relationships, you will have the best opportunity to learn to apply the basics without putting anybody at risk.

As you work with progressively more difficult people, you will become ready to accept the challenge of working with those who have more complex needs. You don't need to begin by working with the most difficult and dangerous cases.

When I start praying for someone, I try to gauge how much trouble they are likely to have when their issues are opened up. I ask them how previous attempts at emotional healing have gone and if they have felt traumatized or overwhelmed while revisiting memories. I look for signs of higher level dissociation and possible SRA. I'm aware that some people on the more severe end of the spectrum will be heavily tempted by suicide if their hurts are brought to the surface. Due to this concern, I don't pray for some people if circumstances aren't right.

I tailor my approach to the level of risk a person's condition could present. I will go more slowly and carefully at first, making sure that people can handle working with their deeper issues without being too overwhelmed.

If someone is likely to have more difficulty, I will take the circumstances of their life into account more seriously. For instance, I don't want to risk someone becoming destabilized and having to show up at a demanding job the next day unable to function. I don't want them becoming overwhelmed in the midst of an already stressful family situation. I also want these individuals to have some type of social and spiritual support systems around them. I don't want them digging up their darkness in isolation if they aren't ready for it.

Don't be afraid to invite others to join you in team ministry, especially in cases that seem "above your pay grade." This sort of ministry becomes much easier with a strong team behind you.

Don't Be Too Caught up with the "Right" Method

You can heal fractured parts in many ways. I've found that different approaches will benefit different people. There is no 'one-size-fits-all' method.

Some foundations remain the same in every situation: Jesus is the answer. He supernaturally removes sins, bondages, and hurts. The parts' issues typically need to be healed before integration will be beneficial. Overt demonic agreements usually need to be resolved, and counterfeit spirits need to be exposed and removed if they are impersonating the Lord to the parts, etc.

On the other hand, each person I work with is a little different. Some people have a lot of parts that need much generational cleansing and deliverance from counterfeit spirits before they are healed. Other people's parts don't need any of that. Some folk's parts need to meet with the Lord so that He can answer many questions and objections before they will receive much healing. Still other people's parts are willing to receive complete healing and integration without ever meeting the Lord.

Some parts need me to answer some of their questions because they aren't comfortable talking with God at first. Some parts need to meet God in the form of a woman, a child, or even in the form of a beloved pet. (I've seen him show up as a family dog before so that He could minister to parts who couldn't receive anything else.)

Some people need their smaller parts healed up first before the larger ones will participate while others need the major, leading parts in their system, such as the Guardian, healed first before the smaller ones receive help. Some start out by healing a child or infant while others start out working with adult parts. In some cases, you can quickly heal large groups of fragments all at once. In other cases, each part must be slowly walked through resolving one issue at a time, part by individual part.

As I'm working with someone, we'll figure out what approach their parts need as we go. I'll tailor the ministry to fit that person's needs. Sessions flow more smoothly and predictably as many of the parts need the same kind of help and even have many of the same issues present part after part. The Lord might lead differently at times, or we might hit a roadblock and need to figure out a new strategy, but once some basics of that person's system are sorted out, much of the process becomes easier.

Sometimes, known methods or approaches fail to bring healing, and I find breakthrough as a result of being led by the Lord in a new direction. Other times, my attempts at being led by the Lord don't help, but experimenting with methods I already know ends up resolving the situation.

Methods and knowledge are not wrong. They aren't enemies of intimacy with God. You don't always have to have a new revelation to be living in intimacy. We can sometimes be religious about this.

The English language is a method, but you can still use it while having a relationship with God. He doesn't demand that you only speak in tongues during ministry because English is a human method. He isn't upset when we use the brains He gave us.

Personally, I'll take breakthrough however I can get it. If a known method brings breakthrough, I'll use it. If a new revelation brings breakthrough, I'll use that, too. I consistently find the need for both.

I've run into some people with a particular step-by-step method that they apply to healing parts with no deviation allowed from one client to the next. Sometimes, that works to a degree, but in other cases, not so much.

I've seen folks rushed through a program of prayer steps and then told that they were totally healed and completely set free simply because they had done the "heaven-revealed" process. Never mind the fact that symptoms of brokenness and bondage remain with fractured parts still talking to the person in their head. They've been through a process that God once revealed to some minister now used by others second-hand, so complete deliverance and integration must have taken place. Any evidence of remaining wounds is said to be a lie from the devil. Looking for more help from another ministry is asserted to be a sign of unbelief and a way back into bondage.

The first concern I have is that this is entirely unrealistic. Nobody is going to be completely healed and set free from every issue through anyone's step-by-step program. We are on a lifetime journey of healing and increasing freedom, and we all have many areas in which to grow. The second concern I have is that people are hurt by this. Many are told that there is only one way to heal and that all other resources are off limits. They might receive some breakthrough from a certain process, but they then stagnate as the method only takes them so far, and they are convinced that it's wrong to continue moving forward.

Our egos like to feel super-powerful as if we have all the answers. We love to think that everyone we pray for is totally healed and delivered. This isn't true for anyone on the planet. People leave every ministry out there with remaining bondages and wounds.

We need to examine the fruit of what we are doing. We need to ask folks what is happening on their end so that we can then realistically evaluate whether our approach actually resolved the issues in question. Just because somebody had a revelation about how to pray for someone once doesn't mean they have the whole picture for everyone's life. Just because someone interpreted Bible principles a certain way, which helped some people, doesn't mean that others don't need another side of the truth.

Don't Wait for Permission from the Pharisees

At times, I've had to make a decision to obey God rather than man as I've stepped out in this kind of healing. I've had to choose between sticking with what was commonly understood and supported by religious organizations or trying to launch out into what I recognized that the Lord was doing, even when I didn't totally understand it myself.

As you begin healing fractured parts, you will most likely need to make a similar decision. You will most likely face resistance from the traditionally minded and will need to just forgive them and continue following Jesus.

When I was younger, I used to "get in trouble" for praying with people. Many of the churches and ministries I came across back then tried to keep strict control over who was allowed to pray for deeper healing, even outside their own gatherings and in the lives of those who weren't part of their groups.

They might have been concerned about someone being hurt or about quality control in ministry, etc., but they were trying to control other people's lives out of fear.

Many folks believed that you needed to be "under church authority" to minister to people or else the angels and the Kingdom of God wouldn't support you. You were thought to be rebellious if you just loved someone and prayed for them without being part of an organized church's program. You were accused of running from accountability and fighting against the system of authority God had put in place.

None of the stories you've read in this book would have happened if I had listened to that type of teaching. None of them happened through being part of a religious organization or church program. I never would have started in many of these areas if I had waited for permission from a church. To even begin, I needed to step out and just start healing people I had relationship with in my own life, regardless of whether church leaders supported that or not.

People literally became upset and accused me of being out of line for helping people. Pastors of a church I didn't even attend warned their followers not to receive prayer from me. They tried to set up meetings with me to bring correction after someone had come to them with a glowing report of their new-found freedom. Even Jesus had Pharisees freaking out when he healed on the Sabbath. He flagrantly broke their rules just to show that God moves outside the box.

Some of the deeper healing ministries I sat under and learned from had all kinds of overly burdensome rules in place. These were successful ministries that each reproduced their ways among teams all over the world.

Some ministries required a certain number of intercessors scheduled to pray whenever you met to heal a person. While intercessors are great, I'm pretty sure that none of the stories of healing I've included in this book involved any intercessors praying during any of the sessions. Is Jesus Christ not our Intercessor with the Father? Can we not minister through the authority of Christ in us?

One leading ministry forbade team members from praying for deeper healing outside their scheduled appointments in their church building. They claimed never to have seen good fruit from such "unauthorized" activities, only disasters. However, all the stories of healing I've shared, all the ministry I do with people around the world today, happens outside a church building.

I've seen mistakes and failures take place outside a church building, but I've also known people who have experienced disasters inside church buildings. Where you pray isn't really that big of a deal. You can succeed or fail anywhere you go.

I've found that people out there have a tremendous need for deeper healing. I can't even pray with most people who contact me because I don't have unlimited time and energy. For the most part, people are left out to dry by traditional religion and not offered any help. This is because very few people have learned to minister in this way.

If everyone is afraid of being out of line, if nobody feels secure about stepping out and healing people, no one will ever become proficient at it. If we all wait for the "established expert" to do the healing, most of the healing will never happen. Many people must begin stepping out and learning through experience if the wounded of this world are to ever find help.

Don't Blame/Condemn Those Who Aren't Healed

When we feel a need to believe we have all the answers, yet someone isn't healed through our ministry approach, it is easy to place the blame on them. We might rationalize this by thinking that they must have hidden sin allowing the enemy to stay, or they must not have enough faith, etc. Similarly, people might share a sin or a struggle that we are tempted to judge them for. When we condemn others for their sins, we haven't yet found redemption in an area in our own lives. We haven't found the love and grace of God for ourselves in that place, so we don't have it to give to others. We must look at where we are condemning ourselves for our own failings and where we feel unworthy of grace.

If we are out healing people, we are probably strong in the areas of loving God, of having faith for Him to move, and of maintaining a devotional life. However, we might minister to someone who isn't strong in these areas. Do we write them off as hopeless because they are angry and blaming God for hardship? Do we write them off because they don't have much faith, because they struggle to maintain a devotional life, or struggle to manage their behavior?

If we are judging people in these areas, we still have our own unredeemed struggles, too. Religious perfectionism can make us feel as if nothing is ever good enough, so we might have many places in our hearts where we become unwilling to forgive ourselves. We must face our own failures and receive the Lord's grace and redemption in those places. This is no small task, but it will prepare us to be a safe place for others so that they can open their wounds.

When working with the severely traumatized, we will meet people with unusually extreme struggles with many things that the average person can easily overcome. We will have plenty of opportunities to have our strongholds of self-condemnation exposed. We might be tempted to judge these people for their more dramatic expressions of problems that we are upset at ourselves about to a lesser degree.

Fear might totally control their life. They might feel powerless and hopeless to a degree that we have never considered possible. Their anger and hatred might be completely out of control. They might find the simplest adult tasks emotionally impossible to perform. We might be tempted to write them off as too far gone.

The easy way out is to respond with condemnation, accusing them of not loving God enough or of finding their identity from their issues and not wanting to heal. If you've been in training or around healing ministry, you might have even been coached about the people you can't help. We might write them off as impossible to heal because they don't have enough faith, have hidden sins, etc. These are the worst things we can do.

Even if those accusations are true about a person, we can still reach them, resolving the woundedness behind those problems. Unbelief can be resolved. A desire to avoid healing can be rooted out of a person's life. Self-pity can be exposed for what it is and miraculously removed. Hatred toward God can be shown to be based on a lie and miraculously removed as well. Shame and fear of coming into the light can be broken down by patient and unconditional love and then completely removed from a person.

An overwhelmingly wounded individual won't likely accomplish these things by themselves. They will need someone who accepts them as they are, who is a safe place for them to be real, and who is willing to walk with them through their pain. They often need someone to believe for them when they don't have their own faith to invite the Lord into those places of brokenness only He can heal.

When we condemn people, we send the message that it isn't safe to be honest with us. We shut people down. We dramatically slow down communication and the process of finding the real roots of problems. An environment free of judgment is essential for deeper healing.

Listening and Building Trust

Don't rush to get things done, take time to carefully listen, empathize, and relate on the human level, even if it threatens to cut down on "productivity."

It takes time to build trust with people. You cannot demand trust or expect it from those with whom you haven't earned it. Even when folks are desperate for help and willing to risk more than they normally would, there is going to be a process of earning their trust before beginning to explore the depths of their hearts.

When you carefully listen to understand someone rather than only to push your views, you are building trust and safety. When you empathize with someone's situation rather than only telling them what to do, you are building trust and safety. When you demonstrate that you can hear about sensitive subjects without judgment, you are building trust and safety.

The book I recommend by Heather Gingrich in the resource section has a great discussion on becoming safe to do this sort of work. She also references a number of other books devoted to this subject. I don't think that growing in this one area could possibly be overestimated. Even if all you did was to become safer, that alone will bring a significant degree of healing to people.

If you come into a session with a hardline agenda of accomplishing such and such in a certain amount of time, and your whole intention is just to make the person jump through hoops toward your goal, the person's heart will tend to shut down. Yes, folks want help, but they also want to know that you can relate to them person to person. Nobody is going to open the deepest areas of their heart to someone who treats them like a project rather than a person. Love opens up people so that they can receive healing.

You cannot rush deep healing. You can only go at the pace that a person's heart is willing to move. Most of the time, moving more slowly will be more productive than going more quickly.

If you are experiencing mysterious blockages to inner healing, you might consider spending some time relating with the person on the human level and building trust. As a person feels more comfortable with you, they often become more open and honest with you and even with themselves. They often begin to understand and to share what is going on inside, their true thoughts and struggles. You will have an opportunity to minister to the real issues, leading to real breakthrough.

Don't Push People to Do More Than They Are Ready For

If God were willing to force people to be healed, He wouldn't need you to help Him. Consider that.

If someone or their parts refuse to do something, such as taking a necessary step in healing, respect that. Rather than attempting to force the issue, try to find a way around the resistance. Look at the underlying reason for it.

For instance, if someone's fractured part is unwilling to let Jesus meet with them because they are ashamed and don't want Him to see them with all their faults, you could reassure them that He bore all the sins of the entire world on the cross and is holding none of it against them. You might seek their permission to have their shame and fear removed with all spirits behind it by a command of authority in Christ before they meet Him. You could find more creative ways to help the part experience the Lord's love a little bit at a time if they aren't ready to encounter it at full blast.

There will be some way to slow down a bit and to resolve the root behind the roadblock. You can continue to make progress while still listening to and treating the part with respect rather than demanding they do everything your way.

If someone's parts are angry and refuse to forgive, you can tell them that they don't have to forgive in their own strength but that the Lord will miraculously take away their anger if they only give Him permission. If they refuse that, you might ask them to share more about why they are angry or why it is important to them to remain angry.

The parts might feel that their anger protects them or that someone needs to speak up about how wrong what happened to them was. You might need to explain to them that they aren't that little child anymore with no means of protecting themselves, but that they are an adult in a totally different life situation. It can help to let the core person share the truth of this with the child part; many years have passed since the traumatic event, and they are no longer who they were; they are no longer vulnerable like they were. They have no need to be concerned about the same thing happening again.

You might need to explain that the parts don't need to hold onto revengeful emotions for the sake of setting boundaries in the future but can do that even more effectively from a place of healing, peace, and clarity of mind if they allow the Lord to remove the anger. This is because removing the anger opens the door to removing the pain and the oppressive strongholds. If they hold onto the anger, they are keeping the woundedness in place, keeping themselves vulnerable to being hit in the same wound over and over. If they let go of the anger, they can be healed so that they don't have to remain a victim.

You might need to explain how remaining hateful doesn't change the situation but only keeps them in pain and bondage. Tell them that it's time to move on and find healing so that they can be a channel for God's grace to make a real difference in the situations of injustice that so concern them.

You might need to resolve some other problem related to the anger, such as the core person not listening to the part or another part's woundedness creating a problem and causing the anger. After you resolve the relational dynamic or the wound that is provoking the anger, the angry part will often be more cooperative. In some cases, you might even need to break a generational or demonic stronghold so that the part can successfully be freed from the anger.

In the worst cases when you just can't seem to convince a part to cooperate with healing a particular issue, it is best to just move onto another area or to hold off for another day. If you try to force the issue, even if you are right, you will destroy trust and only slow down ministry in the future.

Don't Relive Repressed Memories

While working with more heavily fractured parts, you might find them holding memories with which the main personality has lost touch. These might be highly traumatic memories with overwhelming emotions that caused the parts you are working with to fracture in the first place.

I've shared this warning earlier in the book, but I believe it bears repeating. If you try to perform more standard techniques of memory healing in these cases, inviting the person to deeply explore the emotions and details of the newly recovered memory, they will often go into what is called an "abreaction." This means that they will totally relive the trauma all over again, both emotionally and physically. If they were raped and tortured, they will physically experience all the sensations of being raped and tortured once again at full blast. I've seen such a thing happen before and have seen it completely overwhelm a person, causing great instability for a long time afterward.

Some ministries have relied on this technique, which is taken from early psychologists, to integrate fractured parts. Then, they invite Jesus into the memory to bring healing after it has been re-experienced. They think that this is the only way to heal fractured parts.

An abreaction does result in a form of integration. The connections between neurons are reestablished, and parts of the mind become connected where they were disconnected before. Memory is restored to the core person. However, this experience is unnecessary and horrible for the person to endure.

If you discover a repressed, traumatic memory, counsel the person to back out of the feelings and to observe it from an emotional distance. They don't need to be afraid to find out what happened, but at the same time, you don't want the core person intentionally diving into and reliving the emotions, triggering an abreaction. To help them return to the present if they are having trouble backing out of the overwhelming emotions, you might have them examine their physical surroundings or even pinch themselves.

Instead of diving into the traumatic memory, have the part or the Lord verbally identify what emotions and issues they are carrying related to the memory and seek their permission to have the Lord remove them all supernaturally. He can heal and integrate the parts without any need for abreactions.

Even without abreactions, parts and their hosts might experience pain at times as issues are revisited and as they are being removed. The emotional pains and demonic presences don't just disappear but seem to be pulled out of the parts through some sort of process. They might feel the issues more acutely for a moment as that happens. Some people are sensitive enough that removing their most severe hurts momentarily overwhelms them. However, most people don't notice any pain.

I had one of my more sensitive clients ask the Lord what could be done to avoid the pain she was experiencing as some of her deepest hurts were being removed from her parts. The Lord said that He could put the parts to sleep while He removed their pains and then wake them up when it was finished. One of her fractured parts, who had been afraid to participate in healing due to fear of the pain, was then put to sleep, waking up a few seconds later without her woundedness. The woundedness had all been painlessly removed just as the Lord had said.

Since that time, I've used that approach repeatedly whenever people or their parts are concerned that healing will be too painful. With the part's permission, I will have Jesus put them to sleep and remove the issues, waking them up after it's done.

If the parts aren't yet ready to meet Jesus, I will simply make a declaration that they are being put to sleep, having such and such an issue removed, and that they will wake up when it is gone. People are amazed to see and feel a part of themselves go to sleep, waking up a few moments later without the problems they had before. I've even seen this work for Core Identities (Function, Guardian, Emotion).

For those who have trouble even getting in touch with their parts at all due to overwhelming emotions flooding their awareness, I've found it effective to declare beforehand that a barrier is being set up around them so that they won't feel so overwhelmed but will only feel their parts' emotions to a small degree, just enough to be able to communicate them.

Another way to avoid problems is to declare that all traps are dismantled and removed prior to addressing a major demonic or generational stronghold. Sometimes, the demonic sets up devices in the spiritual realm to harm people as soon as a particular stronghold is broken. I've seen these be removed quickly and simply through a declaration so that those strongholds are resolved without any repercussions. It's especially important to remove these booby traps when working with SRA survivors.

Don't Assume Everything Is a Demon but Don't Avoid Deliverance when Necessary

As much as most people would love to go about healing as if the demonic didn't exist or didn't need to be addressed, I find that taking authority over the enemy is necessary in many cases. I don't like to spend my time focusing on demons. I focus on healing the person, but I do use authority in Christ regularly to move the demonic out of the way.

When Jesus sent out His disciples, he sent them all out to heal the sick and to cast out demons. He didn't send some out to heal and others out to focus on deliverance. Healing and deliverance were meant to go together, and the need for one is usually intertwined with a need for the other. You don't have the option to pick and choose based on modern, cultural sensitivities.

If you have any doubt about the application of these things beyond the mission of the apostles, Jesus told them in the Great Commission as recorded in Matthew 28:19-20 to "make disciples of all nations . . . teaching them to obey everything I have commanded you" (NIV). "Everything he commanded them" includes healing and casting out demons. We are meant to continue the ministry of healing and deliverance they started.

On the other hand, many Pentecostal/Charismatic believers assume that every negative symptom is a demon that needs to be cast out. Real life is never that simple. If you hear a negative or accusing thought in your head, that isn't necessarily a demon. It is more likely one of your hurting parts talking to you. This is why you can't cast it out and why it keeps on talking to you no matter how many times you rebuke it. However, it might be several other things as well. You might be picking up on somebody else's issues or thoughts or you might be hearing a disembodied human spirit (familial spirit) who has been passed down your generational line and needs rescuing.

The accusing voice might really be a demon but is most likely a fractured part or one of your Core Identities (Function, Guardian, Emotion). It might be very wounded and trying to "keep you in line" in its own dysfunctional way, using accusations and abuse. It might be under demonic influence or joined to the demonic, needing to be separated from that.

Many times, highly demonized parts at first come across just like demons and might even believe that they are demons. This happens much more commonly than most ministers think. Many are caught up in endless deliverance battles with something that isn't even a demon! It can't be cast out because it's a part of the person that needs to be helped instead.

If you treat your parts like demonic enemies, trying to rebuke them and cast them out in the name of Jesus, you won't effectively resolve their problems. Worse, you will likely hurt the part, causing it to experience rejection and become unwilling to trust you. The part will believe that you are not only unwilling to listen to it but that you verbally abused it when it tried to share its pains and concerns with you. It was most likely only trying to help with something it saw as a problem.

If the parts are small children crying out for help and you aggressively yell at them, cursing them in the name of the Lord, they might be thrown into compounding pain beyond what they are already carrying.

I've run into at least one person who needed to be healed from a decade of severe torment after she went to a Pentecostal service. She was lying on the floor screaming as her parts expressed their pain when the prayer workers there yelled at her parts, trying to cast them out as if they were demons. This "deliverance" event only caused her condition to greatly worsen. The day I met her, I saw that long-held internal pain resolved after only a few minutes of praying over her parts.

If you "cast out" parts, they might go into hiding for a little bit, trying to obey. The voices in the person's head might quiet for a short time, but they always come back. You can't cast out your parts in the name of Jesus any more than you can cast out your liver or your kidneys.

When you are really dealing with a demon, don't let your ego become involved. Your job isn't to be the big toughie that you never were on the football team, stomping on the bad guys with extra gusto. Your job is to love a person and to help them heal, not fight the devil in a cage match.

Jesus already disarmed all the principalities and powers. Even the highest levels of the enemy's kingdom don't have the ability to put up any fight against authority in Christ. If you are experiencing resistance to your commands of authority, it isn't because you need to rile yourself up and yell louder or because you need to flex your muscles and punch the devil in the face to make him go.

If the demons aren't leaving, either they have a foothold that needs to be removed or you don't really believe in your authority. If you believe you need to work yourself up and yell at them, stomp your feet while speaking in tongues, and fast for forty days before they obey your command to leave, then they won't leave until you do all those things. It will be done unto you according to your faith.

In my early days, I became involved in some deliverance activities that were more like fighting the devil than helping the person. Although we saw a lot of dramatic manifestations along with cool, showy demonstrations of authority, I'm not sure any of that helped a single person.

Some poor individual whose life was a mess ended up being along for the ride as demons used their body to swing punches and kicks at us that stopped inches from our bodies, making death threats that never amounted to anything. The body of the host was shoved to the ground at our rebukes, etc.

I even saw one man's body dragged around a room and pushed up against walls as I called angels to fight the demons who had been using him in an attempted attack against me. I tried using spiritual swords and torture devices to drive them out, listening to them scream. They appeared to maybe leave or at least to stop their manifestations before different ones immediately manifested and put on another show. This continued for hours at a time, day after day.

That man's demons were even forced on command to make his bed at night after they kept manifesting and threatening when I pressed them until late hours trying to cast them out. When they claimed to be doing whatever they wanted, including planning to kill me later, I commented that I'd never seen a demon who liked making beds before. All they could do was growl in frustration as they continued doing what they were told, making the bed and putting the body to sleep in it.

I was seeing significant breakthrough in more simple cases, where a demon only needed to be forced to confess a foothold and then removed once the person prayed a prayer of repentance from an issue. However, complex cases involving parts and such were a completely different story. Sadly, I don't know that any of those people received any noticeable progress in real healing or freedom through any of this wild, in-your-face brand of "deliverance ministry" practiced in my earliest years.

These people needed help with the reasons why the demons were there in the first place, not just someone to persistently "battle the forces of evil." At the time, I didn't understand how deep the need for inner healing was, especially for these folks with complex woundedness and many hurting parts giving place to their demonization.

I learned that being caught up in ego battles against demons was only a distraction from helping the person. They love it when we are all worked up and striving against them. I don't think they were insulting me, threatening me, and challenging me in an attempt to win those challenges so much, but in an attempt to get me focused on fighting them rather than on helping the person with the reasons they were there. When taking a fight with the demonic personally, we are not walking in the Spirit and not focused on loving and serving those needing help.

Demons are eager to manifest and torment their host by speaking through them and using their bodies to put on a show. Jesus told His disciples, "Do not rejoice in this, that the spirits are subject to you, but rejoice because your names are recorded in heaven" (Luke 10) for a reason. He didn't want us building our egos on how tough we can be while using our authority over demons. He wanted our hearts at rest, satisfied in the Father's love without any need to perform for our value.

Relate to Parts as People, Not as Objects to be Forced into Obedience

We need to learn the balance between giving parts a voice and being considerate of their needs vs. letting them control our lives.

As people are going through the healing process, we need to listen to their parts, to respect their voice and their value. This is how the Lord treats parts, as real people, not just as something that is preventing healing. He doesn't treat them as objects who need to be suppressed or forced to act against their will. At the same time, we don't want the woundedness of fractured parts running our lives. For instance, we don't want scared five-year-olds making our decisions.

As you are in the healing process, connecting with the emotions and desires of parts, you don't need to let them have their way in every circumstance. You need to be the adult and to lead. Sometimes, you need to do things your parts don't want to do and not do some of the things they do want to do. At times, people don't understand this and let situations spiral out of control, and you might need to counsel people you work with to make hard decisions.

At the same time, suppressing or controlling the parts is not a measure of healing or progress. They aren't meant to be starved of their needs, forced to swallow their pain, and denied everything they want as some twisted version of "walking in the Spirit rather than the flesh." The Spirit doesn't lead us to abuse ourselves.

Rather than shutting down the parts, their needs, their desires, and their voices, people need to learn to build connection with them and to communicate respectfully with them. The goal is healing them, not just controlling them. We want to build trust with them so that we can help them sort out their hurts and thinking with the Lord's help. We want to then invite them to join us again as an integrated aspect of who we are. Don't just see them as a problem but as real people who need to be loved.

Don't Believe Everything People Say, and Don't Take it Personally

When praying with the heavily wounded and with fractured parts, we need to listen to them and to respect their feelings and their voice. At the same time, woundedness is always based on a lie to some degree, based on an interpretation of events and a perspective that differs significantly different from that of the Lord. He went through all the same things at the same time we did, but He is not in need of emotional healing because He had the capacity to see the bigger truth.

People will tell you about events and interactions with others that you have no way of verifying or at least wouldn't want to. You will hear only one side of the story while somebody else's side will often differ greatly. Many times, this is even true when the people on both sides are being honest. Under emotional duress, perception can become very distorted.

We do need to listen to people and honor their views and feelings as true in their own being, which is important for their own process of healing, helping them to meet the Lord and receive His help in the context of these perceptions. However, we also need to remember that not everything they think and feel is objectively true. We don't usually need to decipher the truth in these instances. Knowing what feels true to the person is enough for us to work with.

I've prayed with people who have come to me with horrible stories about every ministry they've ever had pray for them. I've usually found that some truth was in that perspective, that many ministries were overbearing or condemning or giving pat answers that didn't work in the difficult cases. At other times, I've found that the ministries were only sharing what they had been hearing from God, and when I and those partnering with me heard the same thing from the

239

Lord for the person, they categorized us as just another abusive ministry with horrible motives.

I've had some people drastically misinterpret what I said or did while praying for them. I was once invited to pray for a person because others were concerned that they might soon be committed to a mental institution. The person started out more or less incoherent, ranting and raving about all sorts of paranoid, strange ideas. Each session with them produced noticeable change. Many who had known them began to marvel at the transformation occurring before their eyes even after only a brief encounter.

That person went through some heavy emotional upheaval between the prayer sessions and after only a handful, decided that they didn't want to try anything like that ever again. They decided that they received nothing out of our sessions except more pain, despite the fact that everyone else around them seemed to notice dramatic transformation.

I've found that some people have parts who are very resistant to ministry, who will use any tactic possible to sabotage the person's perceptions to make them stop. Sometimes, all the memories of any breakthroughs or positive experiences in healing are hidden away among certain parts whose job it is to obscure them. Certain leading parts only allow the person access to negative memories associated with a ministry or a type of prayer.

The severely wounded will have parts who interpret everything in light of their original woundedness. If they were abused by their father and by men, they will lean toward reinterpreting any interaction with men as predatory. If they were hurt by those who tried to help them, they will tend to reinterpret any attempt at helping as another episode of abuse.

These issues are never resolved by blaming the person or by denying their ability to think for themselves. It truly isn't their fault, but it is the fault of the issue itself. The person truly believes they are doing what is necessary to protect themselves. They need to see the truth for themselves, not be told that they need to throw away their own views and accept someone else's take instead.

I've seen some of these situations turned around by exercising kindness and patience, by consistently acting the opposite of how these perceptions were trying to paint me, showing evidence to the contrary of what the emotionally skewed parts had been telling the person. Enough of this will lead them to begin to doubt the accusations of those parts.

This was never fun. Nobody wants to be accused of harming those they are trying to help, especially when you only see their lives and internal state crashing as they isolate and fight against healing. Nobody wants to be in the thick of someone's pain hour after hour, walking with them through it until finding a breakthrough, only to have all the achieved results denied and even reinterpreted as harm by the only other person who was there.

What's worse is that you might make mistakes and harm people at some point amid such complicated and challenging work, which will really give ammunition to those who lean toward victim/abuser interpretations of every event.

Even worse than dealing with these things in ministry, though, is having to be the person who suffers from those kinds of issues. If nobody will minister to them, they will most likely live the rest of their lives in severe pain, manipulated by the enemy's games. They will never be whole enough to effectively walk out who they are called to be and to exercise their unique giftings. Although it takes a certain amount of maturity and understanding, someone needs to help those in these conditions.

Chapter 24: Seneca

Maintaining Appropriate Boundaries

When you are involved in this kind of ministry, you will go to some deep and intimate places with people. You'll literally go where no man (or woman) has gone before. If you do it right, with the love of God flowing through you, you'll hopefully encounter some extremely love-starved fragments. You'll win their trust, and in that moment, you have to quickly point them to Jesus or they will emotionally attach to you. It may just be a fragment, but it influences the whole person, and he or she might misread those unhealed places as an attraction or a desire to be around you.

If you have any area within you that needs to be needed, sort that out. I have seen too many healers forming long-term codependencies with people to whom they minister.

When Matt was ministering to me, I really appreciated an instance where he had to say, "Nope, not me. Jesus is the One who will never leave you or forsake you." I could feel that part pulling and even though he acted quickly, I still had to deal with it privately after the session.

I'm not going to give you iron-clad rules to follow like formal ministries do, such as never minister alone to a person of the opposite sex. That is not the fail-safe rule that it used to be, and codependency is not necessarily always about romantic attachment. This needs to be a conversation between you and God about who is off limits for you. Your strengths and weaknesses will factor into the situation.

For instance, sensitive guys with wives/girlfriends who invalidate their feelings are a no-go for me because I'm a good listener, and I don't judge feelings. I'm not the one doing life with them and on ground zero with the aftermath from their feelings. The worst thing that can happen is that they hold you up in comparison as a ministry against their other relationships.

I have not found a graceful or pain-free way to shut this down once it becomes an obvious problem, so I fight the tendency to tell myself I have a big head when I see subtle cues that the relationship is becoming inappropriate.

If you catch the issue very early, you can usually course correct by putting a little distance between you in the form of spacing appointments a bit further apart and encouraging them to see other people. I make some referrals based on what I know about the person, and generally after a little time passes, we don't have a problem anymore.

When You're the One With Boundary Issues

A completely different type of boundary issue affects some types of ministers, who have a variety of names: empath, prophetic feeler, highly sensitive person, etc.

These people are drawn to healing and caregiving arenas, and they have a gift for it even though they usually don't like having this gift. They sense everything that everyone else around them is feeling and often struggle with a barrage of emotions from others in addition to their own feelings. Usually, the outside emotions take precedence over anything internal. They take "burden bearing" quite literally, and even strangers recognize that they are a safe "dumping" ground. If they don't learn to work with this, they might commonly develop chronic fatigue or digestive issues. Yes, this is a gift.

I know that extreme sensitivity can cause a lot of pain, but empathy is necessary for people to live in harmony. Empathy bypasses all differences, such as race, social status, age, and anything that serves to divide us. Empathy helps us understand why others act the way they do. Without empathy, we are left with only intellect as a means of understanding, and from there, we move into judgement.

Problems arise when this becomes unbalanced. We don't want our feelings turned off, but we do need to have our boundaries firmly in place. We need to be able to recognize what emotions are ours and what we are picking up from other sources.

I don't have this gift, but for some reason I attract people who do in droves, and I answer questions every day about it. I believe this gift falls under the category of "discerning of spirits" in 1 Corinthians 12. Everything about the gift indicates plurality, which means that it can operate in more than one way. It's not just for those who can see angels and demons in the spirit or for those who have an innate ability to separate truth from lies.

If you need healing in certain areas in your life, you will be especially sensitive to that emotion when you come across it in other people or places. This is called sympathetic resonance.

In energetic terms, this means you'll pick up on other people's emotions more strongly when you have a predisposition toward said emotion. For instance, as an empath, if you have a problem with anger, you'll feel that emotion from others more deeply than you would other emotions that you sense in day-to-day life.

In order to begin learning to distinguish your emotions from those of others, before you enter a situation when you are around a lot of people, or even one or two people with issues, do a personal mood check. Make a mental note of how you're feeling beforehand. If you come out of the situation feeling completely different than how you went in, you have picked up their stuff. If you have an amplified feeling of what you went in with, some sympathetic resonance was probably at work.

Ideally, you'll be able to sort your issues from those of others, pray accordingly, and hand them to Jesus.

You need to be careful that you do not take the emotions all on yourself. It's not yours to carry. Otherwise, you will become a "fixer" who depletes themselves trying to solve everyone's problems so that you won't have to feel the pain anymore. Of course, pain is unfortunately everywhere we look, and you can't fix it all. However, you might be the only one with the awareness to pray with accuracy and intensity. After all, you know how it feels.

I developed the Yarrow Shield flower essence to help people with this kind of sensitivity. It helps strengthen your boundaries and helps with reframing the gift. It doesn't shut down the gift of perceiving other people's issues, but adds an added emotional protection. You'll stay perceptive when working with people without taking their burdens on as your own. I've had testimonies from people who've said that it helps them stand and counteract witchcraft directed at them when ministering to people with occult involvement. A caveat in taking Yarrow Shield if you have DID is that I have one report of it shutting down communication between parts and the core self. However, this person was able to use Yarrow on its own outside of the blend with no issues, so it is unclear what caused the disconnect. See the resource section for more information about flower essences.

Chapter 25: Michael

Transfer Agreements

While we're on the subject of taking on other people's stuff, I want to address the subject of a transfer or a transfer agreement, especially if you are having difficulty freeing someone due to demonic involvement. The theory is that because all demons require some sort of internal agreement to afflict us, whether conscious or subconscious, past or present, if someone is having difficulty getting free, then if we simply move the demon over to another vessel, a human volunteer who lets the demon in temporarily, then we can make progress with the original supplicant. Once the session is done, the plan is to cast the demon out of the volunteer. The idea itself, if it actually worked, is pretty clever as it uses another person as a sort of bait and trap. In spite of the seemingly ingenious nature of this notion, it doesn't work, so let's look at why.

First, just because a demon transfers from one person to another doesn't remove the opening in the first individual. While in theory the goal is to heal that opening, the fact remains that at that point another demon can easily take its place. Now you have two demon-ized people instead of one, and you are no closer to a solution than you were before. Second, the demon, now that you have invited it in, can dig in deep—after all, you very literally asked it to come—and nothing about that is wisdom. Creating openings inside yourself doesn't solve the underlying problem of the other person and only further complicates the situation. You do not become more empowered to set others free by putting yourself under greater bondage, which is the only thing that will happen. Furthermore, when you willingly open up yourself to demons, no rule exists that says you will end up with the demon you were trying to transfer or that you will only transfer that one demon. When they are welcomed with arms open wide, they have a habit of bringing friends along.

What, then, is a better solution? Stay the course. Often, the only answer in a difficult situation is perseverance. Sometimes, continuing what you have been doing is the only way to move forward even as you seek new revelation, wisdom, and increased levels of power and authority. Ask the Lord to bring the right people, information, and circumstances to help resolve the situation swiftly, but under no circumstances should you make a deal with the devil to trade yourself for someone else.

While the argument could rightly be made that the very nature of intercession is to bear and carry something away, Jesus is the burden-bearer, not us. We are to trade His yoke for ours, not one another person's. Besides, assisting with inner healing is a form of burden bearing in and of itself and one that doesn't significantly endanger you in the process, unlike transfer agreements.

Section 4:

The Heavy Stuff— DID and SRA

Chapter 26: Diane

In-Depth Explanation of Alters

From what I understand, the mind is capable of shattering into Dissociative Identity Disorder (DID) prior to the age of six years old, although some experts believe that this capability stops at age three. Once a child's mind shatters, they are then capable of creating alters with each traumatic event for the rest of their lives. The level of dissociation that initially causes DID is extreme and only happens in very serious cases of abuse.

The person must experience an excessive level of cruelty for the mind to shatter initially. After the mind shatters, it takes very little stress for the mind to create other alters. Alters tend to form to handle abusive situations, but I've seen adults create alters to accomplish tasks they didn't want to do: lose weight, do home repair, deal with the in-laws, etc.

If someone comes to you with DID and they claim that they didn't suffer any or very little abuse, know that the abuse is hidden from them by their alters. As you minister to them, you will find the abuse as you lead their alters to healing.

People with DID will have a combination of alters and fragments. Fragments differ from alters and are found in all of us. A fractured part can be caused by trauma or a fracture of our own self, but an alter is a completely different or alternative identity we make. This identity has its own mind, will, and emotions as well as its own name. In DID, clients may or may not have co-consciousness so that they know when different parts are out.

If you have DID, you're made up of different people via alters, but a fracture or fragment is just a part of you that might have been stuck in trauma in an instance of abuse. They are still you, not a different personality. Though you can have a fracture at any age, as stated before, you start developing alters before the age of six.

There are different types of fractures. A fractured mind is like amnesia; the regular mind has amnesia over what happened to that fragment. An alter is a fracture of a different sort. A fractured mind causes amnesia about the self, which is why a lot of people don't remember childhood abuse.

When our mind fractures, it can produce either a fragment or a separate identity, otherwise known as an alter. A fragment is still connected, but a line of divide separates you from your presenting self. You can still access it, but a barrier is there so that you are not normally aware of it.

In what used to be called Theophostic and is now called Transformation Prayer, we were taught that the original child is the part of yourself that experienced the trauma and that this original child will produce a system of alters around them. A comforter might be present to comfort them, like a grandma or a mom. This might even be an animal, such as a kitty cat or whatever comforts them. Protectors, such as a bear, a mean dog, an angry teenager (which is very common), etc., are also found.

Third, helpers carry emotions that the original child cannot carry. They carry the pain, the shock, and the trauma. Various emotions are assigned to these helping alters. One will have the hate. One will have the fear and powerlessness, etc. Each act of abuse can form its own set of alters. Lastly, the gatekeeper alter is the part in charge of the entire system, the personality that decides who is out presenting and when. Permission to talk to a gatekeeper requires great trust, which takes at least the first few sessions to establish.

Once you access the original child and once the abuse it carries is healed by the Lord, the alters connected to the original child will often be healed as well. The original child is circled by layers of alters while a fragment is still connected to the mind but just with a barrier. This is why a fragment can be healed so easily.

The original child is you stuck at the age of abuse, similar to a fragment, but is disconnected from the core person by a layer or layers of alters. The core person, the main identity of the person, is often buried deep within, hiding because the abuse was so extreme, but the presenting person, the personality on the surface, is who they appear to be and who they think they are.

A common example to describe this is that of a shattered mirror. The mirror is cracked, and some pieces have fallen out of it. The cracked portions are still attached to each other and the mirror, but each crack is a part of the whole. It is connected, yet has its own shape. These are like fragments. They are carrying a part of your memory—a negative part.

They are connected yet have their own purpose, which is to help you by carrying the abuse so that you don't have to remember it. The fragments are always stuck in the abuse. They never escape the feelings they are carrying and are very, very tired.

The parts of the mirror that have fallen out are like alters. They might be cracked parts—alters with their own fragments. They are not connected to the mirror. They have their own identity, their own name. They have a story (memory) that they carry that has been made into an entire identity surrounding the memory.

SRA

As far as Satanic ritual abuse (SRA) is concerned, I live in Pennsylvania, which is notorious for numerous cases of this. According to research done by Russ Dizdar of Shatter the Darkness, during World War II, some German immigrants started a camp in Pennsylvania, employing techniques that caused their victims to dissociate and form multiple personalities (Dizdar).

They were experimenting with programming a super soldier with a personality that could be called out to accomplish whatever task they were told to do without guilt or morals affecting it. Supposedly, this camp was located near Greensburg, PA. Shatter the Darkness conducted extensive research into this and also identified a number of "programmers" who were responsible for programming SRA/DID individuals, one of whom was located in Erie, Pennsylvania, where I live.

My first year in prayer counseling, I had eight people with DID. Then, for four or five years, I worked with DID/SRA a lot. Basically, every DID case we worked with was also SRA. We worked with all stages of dissociation: borderline, bipolar, PTSD, depression, and your everyday Christian who was defeated or who had an issue they wanted resolved. We worked with people with tens of thousands of alters, high-level SRA, and programmed people.

We witnessed dramatic events. In the middle of a session, a woman's alter personality surfaced and told us that they were still part of the cult and that this alter was still waking up in the middle of the night, drugging her husband, and leaving to participate in Satanic rituals. Sometimes, she even took her own kids. Another one told us that she was pregnant by an incubus spirit. We wondered if that meant that she was to give birth to an evil plan.

We were cursed by the witch personalities, and we were infiltrated by people from the cult with assignments to destroy the ministry, which was effective. Our ministry suffered accusation and retaliation along with ten other churches in the area as a result of the activity of one woman. Another woman was responsible for bringing division into the ministry and breaking up long-time friendships. The occult does not only send out curses to bring down ministries; they also have "boots on the ground." Some of these are programmed SRA/DID survivors who love the Lord and have no idea they are programmed to bring dissension and problems into ministries.

Cult members also infiltrate the church. They tend to be the "perfect" Christians, usually in leadership or in some cases, the pastor himself, who seem to really want to help and to be "there for you." I've run into many of them. Sometimes, the Lord reveals them to me through discernment, other times, I can tell by their interactions with the survivors.

I was once part of the ministry team in a prayer line, and I heard the Holy Spirit tell me that the person I was praying for did not love Jesus. As I told her that, she took off. She was a witch who had infiltrated the meeting. She was so bold that she entered the prayer line, not realizing that the Lord would out her.

I had one client who had received some healing but who decided to fly across the country as per her cult's demand despite our efforts to stop her. We knew this was so that they could get their hands on her and re-abuse and program her to take her back to her former state prior to ministry.

Her cult was very sacreligious, taking everything in the church and twisting it. Communion was the actual human flesh and blood of a victim they had killed that night. They performed a marriage ceremony where they were married to Satan and became his bride. They spoke in demonic tongues, etc. Her baptism was carried out by her burial underground. Their rebirth was to be sewn inside an animal, usually a cow, and brought through the birth canal.

Some clients had supernatural strength. At first, they spent the sessions flailing on the floor, but I soon learned to take authority over the manifestations. They immediately stopped if they were demonically induced. I no longer allow the enemy to manifest in my sessions because one day, the Lord showed me that most manifestations were just the enemy showing what he could do—like bragging. In some cases, this just strengthens him. I only allow it now as per the Holy Spirit's direction, which almost never happens.

Each alter might have its own blood pressure, its own cholesterol level, and its own eye color. I've seen alters with snake eyes, which let me know that we were dealing with a demonized alter. They can be right- or left-handed or with different prescriptions for glasses while another alter can be present in the same person with no need for glasses at all. One alter might have tumors that appear on a medical test, but if the client goes back for a retest when another alter is out, they have no tumors.

Our minds are capable of these things, which I find fascinating. As medical science continues with its study of our brains, I believe the medical field will develop exercises in which we can take control over our blood pressure or cholesterol levels rather than using medicine. As Christians, we can ask the Lord to teach us how to do this.

Tips for Working with SRA/DID

The first challenge in working with SRA/DID is recognizing that the person has it. Very few individuals come to you with a diagnosis. If they do have a diagnosis of DID, it might take some time before you can identify if SRA is involved because of the amount of denial and hiding by the person suffering from it.

Denial is huge and is usually the first obstacle you face in dealing with DID, let alone SRA/DID. Most individuals have a number of alters whose job it is to create an amnesiac barrier between the presenting personality and the rest of the alter system. Quite often, the presenting personality does not even realize when other alters are present and has no communication with them at all. In these cases, the person experiences little if any co-consciousness, which means that the presenting alter is aware of what is going on at all times even when it isn't in control. Sometimes, the presenting alter feels as if it is behind whoever is in control or at the back of the conscious mind.

Denial's job is to pretend that everything is wonderful, that nothing bad happened. All memories of abuse are denied and covered up. Any presence of alters is also denied and covered up. Breaking down the denial system might initially take some time but is very beneficial. It shortens ministry time when denial is weakened. Denial makes it very hard to have an alter come out for healing. It will take you in circles and throw out red herrings, commonly using confusion and other strategies. The presenting personality becomes confused along with you.

Seek God's direction as to how to deal with denial. Every person who has DID has a different alter system. If they are SRA/DID and have been programmed by the same programmer, then similar systems might operate, but since everyone is different, the pathway to healing will differ.

A lot of denial is programmed into these individuals so that they won't seek help. They believe nothing is wrong, but if they are seeking you out for ministry, then some part of them does know that something is wrong. They might be unable to verbalize what they are feeling, which could lead you to wonder why they are even there. It's very unusual for someone to seek ministry, say that they need help, and then claim that they had a great childhood with terrific parents, and nothing is wrong. This is a huge clue that you need to dig deeper and that DID might be an issue.

You can look for numerous clues that you might be dealing with SRA/DID. If someone tells me that they have few memories prior to the age of twelve, then a huge red flag goes up in my mind. I don't know why, but many SRA/DID survivors will tell me this. It's a huge indicator of it.

Although some of these might just be an indication of DID, they could also indicate SRA/DID. Other signs are missing periods of time since they might not have memories of when another alter is out, or clothes in their closet with no idea of where they came from, especially if they are not the style they usually wear.

SRA folks receive a lot of calls where the caller seems to just hang up. This might be from a private/unknown number or a number that means something to them. I had one case where the phone number included the person's birth date. They run into people who know them but who they don't personally remember.

They have severe emotional issues with no apparent cause, are often a meek, mild person who exhibits times of extreme rebellion and anger, or experience other huge shifts in their character. They might call themselves different names or talk about themselves in third person (she/he instead of me). When asked a question, they have three or four instant answers. If asked their favorite color, they immediately hear red, green, blue, and pink simultaneously. They have a history of harassment from demons. Visits from succubus and incubus are common as well as an unstable home life.

I've even had some tell me that they died for ten minutes and came back to life. This is a particular type of programming where everyone around the person thinks that they have died, but actually, the respirations are so shallow that they are hard to detect. During this time, the mind is being reprogrammed; a program is being installed in the brain. This can happen to someone who has made a lot of progress in ministry. The cult does this to delete what God did and to take back control of the person.

Many SRAs will report receiving phone calls where they think nobody is there. What actually happens is that the person calling from the cult says a code word, a word calling out the alter that they want to talk to. The memory of this is hidden, which is why they don't recall anybody on the other line.

Usually the purpose of the call is to tell the alter where to go so that they can meet up with the cult and be re-abused. The alter they call out is the one who will cooperate and who will go to the meeting that night. Other times, they call out an alter who knows its job is to choose a victim to take to the meeting as a sacrifice. Be ready when you minister to deal with the repercussions the survivor will experience when this is revealed. *Remember*—none of this is their fault! They were programmed, and they are just as much a victim as anyone else in this case!

Most of the SRA/DID survivors that I have ministered to have had a huge revulsion to speaking in tongues. They will become agitated and in some cases, turn violent. However, Matt and I have ministered to one person who we believe has DID. We have no idea if SRA is present, but speaking in tongues has effectively helped her alters to come and receive ministry. They seem to actually understand your tongues and answer them. Many of her alters have received healing this way. It is so easy to just speak in tongues and let Jesus and the alter do the rest!

During my history of dealing with SRA/DID, I noticed three parts of each SRA memory. They have the memory of the ritual performed that night, which might be a sacrifice where raw flesh is eaten and blood drank, or they might be given to Satan in a ceremony, or where some other horrific event happened. Second is sexual abuse: sodomy, rape, child molestation, etc. Third is the actual programming: electro-shock is common where the victims are taken to the point of death and back. The child is commonly forced into fantasy versus reality where the child is shown their reality and a fantasy where they would rather live. This is to force the child to deny reality and live in the realm of fantasy/denial.

Often, those victimized by the occult have a "twin" identity, a powerful "boss" personality. I wonder if it has been a vanishing twin from the womb, another human spirit who was programmed by the cult rather than merely another alter. This seems the same as another presenting alter, but it is not. They might switch back and forth on you. At times, demons might also pretend to be an alter.

Some alters might believe that they themselves are demons. They will act like demons, but I can tell the difference by spiritual discernment. Also, as you gain a feel for this type of ministry, you will sense something about them that is different from a demon. You just know they aren't a demon even though they continually insist they are.

One way I let them know that they aren't a demon is by using my authority in Christ. If it were really a demon, it would be prohibited from operating in the name of Jesus, etc. I look into their eyes and directly tell them that they are not a demon, that they couldn't be or else they wouldn't be talking to me anymore. I work to convince them of this truth so that they can begin to receive healing.

The cult is very good at tracking their victims. They cannot move anywhere without being tracked and manipulated. Even if they change their phone number, the cult learns it, probably from one of the alters snitching. They end up connecting with cult members when they join new churches or move to new neighborhoods. They find that cult members are living in the new neighborhood or even teaching classes at their new church. They are still being abused, programmed, and assigned to do jobs for the cult.

Working through the system takes time, but if you can find the alter who is being used for this, who is responding to the phone calls, you can minister to that alter and bring healing so that the cult can no longer use them in this way. I've known some ministers who have guarded the residence and prevented the client from leaving until they were free enough to not be available for the cult to manipulate in this way. Once the alter who had been going to the meetings was healed, agreeing to the activities was no longer even a consideration.

Some families have many generations in the Satanic cult and have become very competent at what they do. They are very knowledgeable and skillful at operating in the spiritual realm, at moving in spiritual power, and at abusing and programming their victims psychologically. They have learned to program and train people to operate in the spiritual realm with great understanding and clarity of perception. They can cause their victim to have photographic memories through the programming they do, along with developing other unusual abilities.

These people are programmed to live in a make-believe world from a young age. For instance, they are offered a beautiful Thanksgiving dinner, but a dead body is in the corner of the room, and the child is forced to act as if nothing's wrong. They are taken to the corner and made to eat parts of the human body, then brought back to the Thanksgiving dinner. The idea is to twist their perceptions of reality so that they are used to functioning as if everything is fine even while all the abuse is happening in their lives. This also creates the system of denial in the child.

Some of our SRA clients were abused by their own family members. Some of these family members were not only leaders in their cult, but pastors of apparently thriving Christian churches as well. They intentionally infiltrate the churches, deceive people, and gain positions of leadership. One of these churches was in my area, and people constantly testified how great the church was and how God was apparently moving. I have personally worked with one person who reported these events.

The enemy doesn't seem to care much if people are born again or if they go to a nice "anointed" church. Every child abused by the cult is born again early on in their rituals because it increases their capacity to do what they are doing in some way. The child's spirit might possibly be tenderer after salvation, making it easier to manipulate and program them more effectively. The cult definitely has a purpose for doing this. It might be done so that the person will seek out churches where they can then be used to create disturbances and hinder the work of the Lord.

At some point, a multiple, especially a higher level one, will often turn on you. This can happen no matter how effective you are, no matter how much healing they have received. They might tell you how wonderful you are every day for six months and then accuse you of whatever they can come up with. Even though their accusation will have an element of truth, it is usually off-base. This is part of the disease—they are blinded by the issue itself and don't realize what they are doing. They might spread accusations to others and do a great job of making it sound totally innocent on their part. Be prepared for this. Never minister to a multiple alone. Always have a witness, an intercessor, or somebody else there.

If you work with someone who is SRA, realize that you might be working with someone who has alters who are still active in their cult. They might be fulfilling assignments from their cult while other parts of them are receiving ministry. If you aren't healed in any area, be ready to be triggered. First, be ready to deal with your own issues.

Be aware that this information is only a small part of what you will face when dealing with SRA/DID. I recommend that you go through further training before attempting to minister to these folks. I learned a lot from the *Advanced Theophostic Training SRA/DID* class as well as from Restoration in Christ Ministry's DVD training. A lot of excellent training modules are out there.

Tips for Healing Fractured Parts

You can heal fractured parts in many different ways, but the common denominator is that you have to introduce the part to Jesus and allow Him to do the healing. The problem can be convincing them to see or hear Him. You can do that in different ways. A multiple can see the Lord and connect with the Lord so much more clearly than we usually can.

Early on, the person and their parts should create a safe place within where nobody else is allowed to bother them. They can make this safe place within just by using their imagination. Make boundaries/rules/guidelines for the safe place. Nobody is allowed to harm the parts who take refuge there. Nobody can retaliate against them, hassle them, etc.

Many of them receive a lot of retaliation from demons or from other programmed alters when they share information. They need somewhere to go to escape from that. The safe place can be a house, a beach, a forest, a garden, or whatever gives them peace. They can meet with Jesus in this place if they want.

I tell the person that their parts can connect with Jesus. I encourage the person to develop this on their own. I will call forth the inner child or the specific age the Lord has given me through discernment, and they will often come out and talk.

Many people use diagramming to map out where they've been in previous sessions, including who was healed and who wasn't. Parts can let you know who is there and who is connected to whom among the parts. Mapping out the system of alters and their different groupings in this way can help you keep them straight. The setup differs for each client. Some have a house; some have a castle, etc. You can keep records of who is a Protector, a defender, a helper, what job they do, who is programmed or not, who has received Jesus and who hasn't. Make notes when various parts integrate to track that, too.

For instance, one SRA client had three sets of pyramid structures that we had to map out. The cult designed this after the Egyptian religion, connected to Isis, Osiris, and similar Egyptian spirits. The pyramids were partially underwater with various fractured parts and alters in different sections of the pyramids. If a section of the pyramids was above water, the woman could access the parts in those sections. When sections of the pyramids were underwater, she was oblivious to those.

I'll often call whoever wants healing among the parts together to the Lord. I have them look at their back to see if anything is on it. Some have had iron spikes in their back, visible demons, dark spots, etc. Typically, anything on their back is demonic, so I have the Lord remove and heal it. Introduce them to the Lord and ask the Lord to heal each one of them. Sit back and watch Him do it. I've seen as many as fifty to a hundred parts healed at once this way. This doesn't work for all alters in every situation, since, let's face it, nothing does, but quite a few will be healed.

In one situation, a client was having trouble going to church because she had an alter who didn't like going. This part acted up every time. We negotiated with this alter, offering her a treat she especially liked if she behaved when the client went to church. The part stopped being disruptive and received a treat after every church service. You can work with child parts just like you would with a kid. Many of them respond to dolls, coloring books, and other toys. Use them as needed in ministry.

A whole book could be written on different ways to minister to alters. The more you know, the more you will be able to help them because one way doesn't always work for everyone.

Borderline personality disorder is another dissociative condition. They have a positive part and an evil part. They tend to have a very difficult time seeing the Lord. They are hard to heal because when the positive part is healed, this doesn't translate over to the evil part. They know if the good or bad part is "out." At times, they seem to be two different people. Sometimes these individuals are diagnosed with DID because of this, and other times those with DID are diagnosed with borderline. Always keep an open mind when dealing with someone who comes to you with a diagnosis. Follow the Lord's leading and not man's diagnoses.

Chapter 27: Ruby

Coming Out of the Bonds of RA and Freemasonry

I have asked myself, "Am I crazy? Am I making this stuff up?" I was pregnant with my second child twenty-six years ago when I began having disturbing dreams and even nightmares. Later, these were followed by flashbacks to childhood memories that intruded into my thoughts during the day. Whatever had previously held back my buried past seemed to have broken loose like a dam.

Growing up, I had suffered from many years of depression that increased after puberty. I went to counseling and was on medication for depression. At fifteen, I told my mother that I didn't like myself even to the point of being suicidal. My adolescent years were troubled, and I coped by overeating, striving, and people pleasing. Layers of fat hid my pain and made me a social outcast with most of my peers. The war with myself escalated. As my weight increased, so did my self-hatred. I cycled through diets, self-help books, and later, religion.

In the summer of 1984, my life changed forever the day I met my husband. I believe it was a divine appointment. God sent someone to love me. Our journey together has not been easy, but it is a story of hope and love. I came into this marriage a very broken person. I was fragmented and dissociating, but I didn't understand it at the time. I always had many conversations going on inside my head and thought that this was normal. I assumed that my brain just worked faster and differently than some people. It was a challenge, but we learned to communicate as different "parts" spontaneously surfaced. Later, as I began to realize when a "part" was going to switch, I blurted out, "Changing gears!" to warn my husband the conversation was going change.

I am not sure what triggered the dam breaking that I mentioned earlier. I've been told that suppressed trauma often begins to surface in women in their mid to late 20s and that's when walls begin to crack and then finally shatter. Was it the pregnancy? Or was it because I was eight months pregnant when I was baptized? I do not know for certain. What I do believe is that God came to heal my broken heart to make me whole. It's been a long journey as I am now fifty-three.

This cycle of depression and mania continued for many years. I made the rounds for years with secular counseling and medication for depression. I was attending a church that believed the gift of the Holy Spirit had ceased. I was on the brink of suicide many times. During my third pregnancy, I went to inpatient mental treatment and was diagnosed as bipolar. After the birth of my third son, I was flat-line depressed, living on the couch as nonfunctional although I rallied for a short time.

About eight years later, I connected to a Bible study group with people who prayed in the Spirit. I went to a church that was more sensitive to moving in the Holy Spirit and to following His leading. I was baptized in the Holy Spirit, which began the power of God flowing in my life.

In 2006, I went on a mission trip to Guatemala. I was praying for people in a church, and the power of God hit me like an energy bolt of lightning while I was speaking in tongues. I heard the Lord say, "I am going to make you a conduit for healing." I had no understanding for this experience, but it changed my life. I felt the tangible power of God although I did not realize it at the time.

When I returned, I shared this experience with a lot of "Christian" friends. I asked, "What happened to me?" I seemed to hit a nerve with them and found it a bit ironic that they believed in the power of God without recognizing it or wanting anything to do with it. I was labeled a weirdo of sorts. I began to hear from God more clearly and had dreams and visions. I continued seeking to find believers who could relate to what I was experiencing.

After two years, I found someone who said to me, "Oh, God wants to use you to heal people. Go to the Healing Rooms." I made my first visit to the Healing Rooms in 2008. The supernatural nature of God began to open up to me and set my heart on fire for more. I had a longing to be whole and was introduced to the word SOZO here. I began to understand that I was a three part being: spirit, soul, and body. My soul was broken.

There, I first started dealing with parts. They had people who recognized that I was fragmented, which was the first time I heard about it. They started helping me. Their methods are different than what I use now, but they did help me learn, for one, that parts were real, that I could learn to communicate with them, and that Jesus would show up to help. It was an introduction that helped me and that worked. I understood the basics of fragments.

When I arrived at the Healing Rooms, I had already recovered many memories of childhood trauma: sexual, emotional, and physical abuse by my father, grandfather and an uncle. As the memories progressed, I started having memories of sexual abuse that were attached to the memories of rituals. The subject came up when I was in a safe place. God brought up memories so that I could process the memory with the help of the Healing Room team. They were very generous with their time and often stayed late or scheduled an extra-long appointment of nearly an hour instead of the usual fifteen minutes for me.

After a few years, I seemed to reach a point where I needed more support than they could provide. A few people didn't understand why I was still having problems and issues. I was becoming frustrated. Sometimes, when people don't understand what you are going through, they will throw the problem back in your lap. One of the things I was told was that I was giving the devil too much credit and that I needed to take more authority. While there was probably some truth to that statement, I didn't understand my identity or my authority. As a fragmented person, I needed compassion. Thankfully, I didn't let those words discourage me. I kept pushing through, and God brought the people I needed who were willing to listen to me.

In 2011, God brought a kindred spirit into my life. He had experience working with people who weren't finding help in the traditional "Christian" church. We processed through three years of finding fragments and bringing them to Jesus. We started having these journeys where they were hidden or needed something or needed demons cast out. I then had deeper memories that were attached to ritual abuse. It was a journey of remembering. God is really good. Unless it was necessary to heal a fragment, I did not need to remember or visualize details. Jesus did not nor would He ever re-traumatize me.

I have learned that God reveals to heal. I had an enormous amount of fear about digging through my past. I was concerned that I would have to remember all the abuse. It was difficult and painful to realize that the people who should have protected me had used me. I went through periods of shock and denial followed by anger, bitterness, feelings of abandonment, betrayal, grief, and sadness. I believe that many survivors go through these cycles.

Learning to process all those suppressed feelings overwhelmed me at times. I used a lot of tools, such as keeping a journal, walks on the beach, and occasionally, retreating to my bedroom to scream into my pillow. I am so thankful for those who just listened or hugged me and did not try to fix me or minimize my pain.

As I continued my journey I discovered what I am calling "an age of accountability." This applied to my parts who were twelve years and older. I found that God just came in and healed the babies and younger fragments. Often, parts were being held captive, and Jesus brought up a memory or took me to a place in the spirit to rescue these parts. I often got in touch with feelings associated with the trauma, and, after giving the feelings to Jesus, I experienced emotional and physical healing on some level.

Again, I experienced healing in layers. Many times, fragments did not know or trust Jesus, but He used different methods to gain their trust. He might tell them a story or show them where He was when something bad happened. My older fragments exercised their free will more than the younger ones. This is my understanding of the age of accountability. Older parts were nurtured by Jesus' love. As love and understanding grew, they were empowered with choice. Sometimes, this was a quick process. Other times, the part needed more time to heal.

The point is that each one was treated with compassion and patience. When they were ready, they learned to come out of agreement with whatever was done to them. I took an active role in helping my fragments, and in a way, it was like being my own parent. I taught them about who they were and why they existed. Jesus was with me the whole time, guiding me, coaching, and loving me.

Forgiving has been a big part of the process. I could forgive for the parts that were too young to do it themselves. I have discovered that forgiveness is not necessarily for the other person but more for me and my healing. God has orchestrated this whole process in a creative order that I did not always understand.

As I continued to work with the healing counselor, he recognized memories that seemed to point to RA (Ritual Abuse). It was like having the missing pages in a book returned to me. As parts returned and were integrated back into my core, I began to see a bigger picture.

I am not even sure this fits the normal profile for RA if there is such a thing. My parents were involved in some type of swinging sixties groups. Mainly, my abuse happened at parties with lots of drugs, alcohol, and sex. Was this some type of witchcraft or Wiccan group? Were the parties a cover for the evil activities they were doing?

I do have memories of rituals and of my involvement. This has been a lot to sort out. I have also most recently recovered fragments that were abused by my parents' involvement in Freemasonry. We also had neighbors who were into occult practices. This man was a professor; he and his wife practiced this dark stuff. I believe they hypnotized and drugged me. I believe that some of the abuse happened during these wild parties and that I was subjected to some type of mind control. I was indoctrinated at a young age.

After that, I remember being taken to another neighbor's home where they were practicing voodoo. We also had a "hippie" neighbor who read palms and crystal balls and conducted seances. All my fragments involved in these activities were later taken through healing and deliverance to break off the occult agreements and curses. We asked the Lord Jesus to come and then a memory or fragment surfaced. We did what was needed for them to be healed and set free.

During one of the initiation rituals as a child, I went from being an observer to becoming a "member." I was coerced by threats of violence to family members, especially of harm to my younger siblings, so I "agreed" to the ceremony. They "laid hands" on me. I believe this was when a counterfeit Holy Spirit entered my spirit and started controlling my mind. I also believe this activated what some people call the "third eye" or the "psychic door." I began to realize that this spirit guide was a demonic creature that obstructed me from wholeness. It was a gatekeeper of sorts, affecting me spiritually, emotionally, and physically.

One day during a healing session, we decided to try something different. Instead of calling up a fragment, we called my spirit to attention. This was the first time that I became aware of my spirit as a part of me. I learned to communicate with her much like a soul fragment. My spirit was in chains, and she was quite sad and discouraged. I watched as Jesus and some of His angels set her free, resulting in euphoria for me.

After that, more fragments started breaking loose as my activated spirit started participating in my healing progress. She often had clues or other information that was helpful in the recovery of my soul's parts. Although this was a step in the right direction for me, I was just seemed to be cataloging more fragments. After three years, it felt as if this process was never going to end. I was becoming frustrated again. I was trying to "trust" the process, but I began to wonder what I was missing.

I was seeking wisdom from God, and He answered. I was connected with a group of believers living outside the walls of the institutional church and began to attend their "gatherings." I found a safe community where I was accepted and began to grow again. They hosted an event with Mike Parsons about two years ago. I had no idea who he was or if I should attend. I shared a word of knowledge and a vision with a few of my friends, which confirmed God's call for me to attend.

I then started learning about my function in the kingdom and my identity in Christ. I learned that I could step through the veil and be led by my spirit. I had to realign my mind set. I had always asked Jesus to come even in the earlier work of activating my spirit. The thought never occurred to me to go up, to ascend to heaven. I believe I was operating in the spirit to the degree I understood, but now I had become intentional about it.

I began listening to Mike Parsons' teachings and learned to "engage" with God. I was on a personal journey of intimacy with Father God, who I usually call 'Papa' since I've had a lot of father wounds. Now I know that I can activate my imagination to see in the spirit through the veil, go to my mountain of authority and sit on my throne and see my identity in Christ. This has made an enormous difference in my healing.

All my reality was previously filtered through my broken soul, but God's desire was wholeness for my soul. As such, God began teaching more about communication spirit to spirit with Him. I do not completely understand the complexity of the relationship between the spirit, soul, and body, but activating my spirit began to help me function more clearly. I was able to have a higher view, I guess you could say, as my mind was renewed.

The Bible tells me to "seek first the Kingdom of God, then all these things will be added to me" (Matthew 6:33) and to "lean not on my own understanding, but acknowledge Him in all my ways, and He will direct my paths" (Proverbs 3:6). This has been a journey into the heart of Father God, entering like a child to be nurtured so that I could learn to see and hear in the spirit. This took some time, practice, and effort on my part. Now, I make no separation between heaven and earth as I live in both realms. My spirit's senses and redemptive gifts are activated from heaven to earth rather than activated from the earth to heaven.

I am a spirit being who has a soul and body designed to function together in completeness. I am uniquely and wonderfully made, which is an amazing mystery to me. I have discovered that reading Psalm 139 out loud to myself is very healing. I change the pronoun and put my own name into the passage instead. I believe the Bible is God's love story with His children. In my experiences, He is still speaking and sharing revelation. For me, the Bible is a starting point, and there is always more for me to learn and experience with Father God in my own personal relationship.

I wondered about peace, specifically what I read about it in Scripture: "the peace that passes understanding" (Philippians 4:7). I wanted that kind of peace! I found it in the realms of heaven. I love to go into the throne of grace where I climb up into Father God's lap.

Sometimes, I see Him as a gentle loving Grandfather, and He rocks me in His arms and sings to me. It is a safe place of love and restoration. He is never too busy and is always available for me. He delights in me and looks forward to my visits. As I soak in His love, I stop striving. In this place of rest, I bring my cares and surrender them to Him. I can process a memory or various emotions. I can release the fear, worry, or any emotional burdens. I deal with anyone or with any situation that I need to forgive. Often, I need to forgive myself. I find peace and healing. I am not always aware of what has transpired, but I am being transformed spirit, soul, and body.

I am in the process of cleaning out the gateways of my spirit, soul, and body as well. I suggest reading Ian Clayton's book, Gateways of the Threefold Nature of Man for more information about this. Healing trauma in my gateways has allowed me to function better overall. These blockages are sometimes attached to trauma experienced by my fragments.

Sometimes, God will show me a blockage that needs to be cleaned out. I was having trouble understanding a situation once, and I messaged Seneca, asking her if there was a flower essence to help me. She, of course, answered, "Well, that depends on what is going on." After talking with her, I heard the Lord say that I had an issue with feeling hopeless, a blockage in my hope gate.

Seneca recommend that I try taking New Hope Music Essence. After taking the flower essence, I went in the spirit, and the Lord showed me what was blocking my hope gateway. Many times, I simply needed to repent or have a lie exposed, following the Holy Spirit's lead to clear out the blockage so that flow can be restored a gateway.

I will give a brief testimonial here about flower essences. I met Seneca about nine months ago, and began using different flower essences at that time. I believe using them has significantly accelerated my healing, especially in my emotions. I have been able to process on a deeper and more restorative level. I have been chasing around these feelings for years but am finally making my way out of the maze. I had so many issues that I decided to go with a custom combination, which I highly recommend. It is like having an emotional healing partner. Seneca has an extraordinary gift that has blessed me.

In the process of working through my healing from heaven's perspective, I came to realize that my spirit wasn't completely healed. It wasn't just that my soul was full of trouble. I had issues with my spirit, too. My spirit was fragmented, fractured, and not fully functioning, which was part of the reason that I wasn't experiencing breakthroughs. My spirit needed healing so that it could help heal my soul and body.

I believed the fallacy that I was taught: once you accept Jesus, your spirit man is made perfect with no further problems with your spirit. Not everyone has problems with their spirit, but because of ritual abuse, including Freemasonry, my spirit was damaged. I missed the issues going on in my spirit for a long time due to the belief system that I mentioned.

Again, God came in and renewed my mind to bring understanding and awareness. I believed my soul was horrible and no good. I've discovered that isn't true. God created the soul to be good. It is wounded, but it isn't bad or designed to be a scapegoat or something for me to loath. My body is not bad. I still struggle with my body image. I have difficulty loving my body and seeing it as a beautiful creation. I am currently on a journey to fully accept, love, and cherish my body. God created it all as good: spirit, soul, and body.

I have also learned to trust myself. If something does not sit right with me, I ask questions. My ideas and voice were ignored and minimized for so much of my life. I am doing my best to be gentle with myself.

I'll list some teachings that I do not completely agree with: telling my soul to submit to my spirit and the further suggestion that I divide my spirit and soul. I did not find this helpful to my hurting soul. I was not going to force my soul or body to submit by yelling at them. The Lord had me repent for considering my soul as the wicked stepmother and my body as the ugly stepchild.

The Father, Son, and Holy Spirit lovingly guide and direct me. I have learned about the alignment of my spirit, soul, and body and am learning to function in wholeness. I have also begun a process of blessing my spirit, soul, and body. I have been using Arthur Burk's book, Blessing Your Spirit.

David Tensen from Leader's Heart Ministries also has some excellent materials, including a soaking CD for blessing. I have been learning about the redemptive gifts of my spirit, how they function, and the role they can play in helping to heal my soul and body. I am still processing through my spirit's redemptive gifts. Christian ministers Mike Parsons and Arthur Burk have wonderful information on the redemptive gifts. You can find some of this information on YouTube.

More recently, I have discovered how much Freemasonry played a part in my bondage. A couple of weeks ago, I was talking to my fragments. I asked why I was hurting and, "What's going on?"

A fragment answered, "The wizards are mad at you because you are not doing what they want you to do."

I asked them to tell me what that was all about. Later, a memory surfaced involving a Masonic temple, and I saw a hoodwink ritual. The next day in a healing session, I recovered more information. I had an encounter with Jesus, and he told me to look inside my pocket. I discovered a Masonic ring. I handed Jesus the ring, and he shared some key information with me. I then realized it was time to start digging for more answers.

For about six months, God kept dropping hints about Freemasonry into my path. I downloaded information and even ordered the book by Grant and Sam Mahoney called Freedom: Coming Out from under the Curses of Freemasonry. It sat on my desk. I picked it up and then put it down again. It seemed too overwhelming to begin.

After my encounter with Jesus, I made another effort to read it. Every night, I read the book and worked through a few degrees, which are the steps of advancing through Freemasonry. As the curses were broken off, I found myself going through a self-deliverance process. I used prophetic soaking music and deliverance prayers that I found especially useful, such as the "Command the Morning" prayer by Dr. D K Olukaya.

I had been through some deliverance before, so I was not too surprised when I was gagging and coughing up things, and the swelling in my abdomen even subsided. I had been to the doctor because

I suffered with physical pain, but they couldn't find anything wrong. I realized that this was a spiritual attack. I had a revelation that, as the firstborn child, all the Freemasonic curses landed on me after my dad died in 2012.

In hindsight, I can look back to when my health took a turn beginning in October 2012. I previously believed this was because I was already on the healing journey. Working through the book shed light on exactly what I was dealing with and how the curses had transferred to me and had started manifesting in my life.

A lot of crossover occurs between Freemasonry and RA. My understanding has changed, which has cleared up some of my confusion about my childhood. My memories are sort of like snapshots in time. I spent a lot of time worrying that I was making up events. I was repeatedly called a liar. Cults are based on keeping secrets, whether it is a Wiccan coven or Freemason brotherhood. Mind control, gaslighting, fear, and manipulation are major tools. Is it any wonder that I splintered into pieces?

What the enemy meant for evil, God made to protect me and keep me alive. Now, I have other memories that are connected to Masonic rituals. I have had many snapshots of all manner of evils done to me at the hands of people that I loved and trusted. I am not so concerned about who and why anymore but more about the what. What am I going to do with the information and revelation that I have been given?

I believe that my dad's involvement with Freemasons opened the door to evil. My uncle, who I mentioned earlier, was also a Freemason and involved in the occult, and my aunt was high ranking in the Eastern Star. I have also discovered that this has been a bondage in my family line going back many generations.

My dad wanted a son, and he made a trade with the enemy for me if he could have a boy. My mother conceived a son but suffered a miscarriage. Satan does not keep his promises but replaces them with lies, false power, and destruction. My family paid a high cost.

Regardless of how or where or what opened the door to evil, evil is evil, and grading it hasn't helped me heal. At times, I found myself stuck trying to find answers. None of it makes sense neither did it excuse the behavior. I have chosen the path of forgiveness. I do not say this lightly. In my experience, forgiving is not easy but is a process. I have found healing and freedom in forgiving.

I believe it is important to mention that many people do not know about the influences of Freemasonry. Many of the founding fathers of the United States were Freemasons, and they used Masonic principles that were woven into the governmental system. After doing some of my own research, I was shocked by these foundational principles. When I closely examined them, I discovered these same ideologies in many other organizations, such as: fraternities and sororities, Elks, Moose, Kiwanis, Shriners, Girl Scouts, Boy Scouts, Knights of Columbus, Foresters, and Eastern Star.

I was a member of Girl Scouts from age seven to twenty-two. A lot of deception is involved as the enemy did not want me to know the truth. I was programed at a young age, which desensitized me so that I did not recognize anything wrong. I believe Freemasonry is just more of a socially accepted form of the occult with a pretense of doing good. They promote one image, but much evil is done in darkness for power, money, and prestige.

Because of my involvement in Girl Scouts, and even as a citizen of the USA, I made promises, oaths, and allegiances. God showed me that even saying the Pledge of Allegiance is aligning myself with something other than God. I am a citizen of heaven. I am not anti-American, but I did not realize the power operating behind these oaths. I believe they are tethered to the demonic.

God says not to have any other God before Him. Anytime I make an agreement outside my covenant with Him, that is what I am doing. I take time now to examine the motivations of my heart. I ask Father God to search me and know me, to see if there are areas of darkness with which I have unknowingly come into agreement. God is a loving Father to me. He is not angry or surprised by anything. This is one way that I am untangling the trauma from ritual abuse.

I did find freedom from breaking curses. This did not resolve all my issues but removed more layers. The most exciting thing to happen was a few days after I completed the book on Freemasonry by the Mahoneys. While I was breaking off the curses, fragments that had been taken captive were set free. I asked Jesus to send angels to bring back any parts, heal them, deliver them, and reintegrate them when they were ready.

The first couple of days when I started breaking the curses, I was overwhelmed. I was aware of a bunch of fragments. It was like having thirty new kids show up for class, but they were too young to pay attention. I couldn't accomplish anything in my healing sessions, so I decided to send them out to recess to be with Jesus. I said, "Okay, everyone who wants to go outside and play, Jesus is waiting for you, and I will talk to you later." Suddenly, things grew quiet as they went with Jesus. I could focus again.

Later that day, I gathered all the ones who would listen, and I told them the story of us. I shared all about the terrible events that had happened to them, how they came to be a part of me, and that I was sorry for what happened to each one. We then gathered around Jesus in a grassy field. I continued sharing my journey and relationship with Jesus and about how He died on the cross for me, that God loved me and sent Jesus to heal me and set me free.

I also explained that they did not have to hold onto hurts and physical pain. I wanted to give my fragments permission to release those things. This was a healing session for all those parts, and Jesus gave them all a mirror, telling them that they were beautiful and that He loved them. They got to look in the mirror and see themselves as Jesus saw them—beautiful and beloved. In the end, they chose to let Him enter their hearts. They shared communion, went with Him, and I slept for an hour as those parts were integrated back into my core.

This was the beginning of healing my body image. I believe physical healing will come out of this, too. Jesus gave me an assignment that day to begin looking at myself in the mirror. He asked me a very hard question, "Are you done hating yourself?"

I first heard the term, "alien human spirit," a few years ago, which is also known as a "disembodied human spirit." I was wondering if I could be holding someone else's parts. While I feel I have more to learn in this area, I discovered that I had fragments who were not mine.

Sometimes, these fragments come from unhealthy soul ties that need to be severed. Occasionally, this will pop up. One of my Guardian parts said, "I have been taking care of this part for a long time, but she doesn't look like you." It was then revealed that this was a part of my cousin. I have had parts of my sisters. I have simply released them back to Jesus. It was bizarre.

I had parts who thought they were demons and demons have lied about being fragments. The enemy wants to bring confusion. Jesus is my best friend, my Healer, and the Restorer of my soul. I still do not understand so much, so I often ask Jesus to take anyone that the enemy has planted in me back to where they belong or to a safe place.

I found very valuable information on DID, SRA, and Freemasonry from Dan Duval at Bride Ministries. He specializes in helping people in high level bondage. I have incorporated some of his teachings to help with issues that were not responding to my usual methods. This is where I learned about "abominations." Abominations are humanoid creations made from human DNA. The enemy can plant these beings into people during rituals. Because of my history, I began to ask Jesus to reveal any abominations and to destroy them.

These are not human souls. I have mercy on human souls but not on demonic creations. I find these critters are destroyed by the refiner's fire or water from the river of life. Dan Duval also has some prayers that I used to help break related agreements and bondages.

I was created for relationship, and having a tribe of people has been vital to my healing. My husband has been my biggest support. I have had some difficult things to share, and I needed safe people who believed me and stood by me while I walked through this stuff. I do not recommend taking this journey alone.

Walking through this process has been hard, but I have not given up despite discouragement. I used to see my healing as a destination, but now I see it as a journey. I have been developing an intimate relationship with Father, Holy Spirit, and Jesus. I couldn't have done it without them. Jesus is my best Friend. The Holy Spirit gives me wisdom. Father God patiently loves me. I am not alone. He will never leave or forsake me.

I was a bruised and broken person, but God has put me back together again. One of the pastors at the Healing Rooms said I was like Humpty Dumpty—shattered and broken. God didn't just put my broken parts back together again; He made me whole. He didn't just fix up the old, damaged me. He made me new, and He is still doing it. I have experienced hope and freedom. My heart's desire is to see others who are suffering healed and set free. I did not know where to turn and did not find help in the institutional church, but God made a way for me. I found love and peace. My journey continues one day at a time. God's mercies are new every morning. Great is His faithfulness to me!

The Authors and Their Resources

Sam R. Brewster

Sam, who is using a pseudonym for various reasons, has trained and worked in the field of inner healing for several years. The ability to heal fragments was an interesting discovery that has helped many clients. Sam hopes that you find the information in this book beneficial on many levels.

Ruby Hunter

Ruby Hunter lives in the Pacific Northwest with her husband Joseph. She has been married to the love of her life for thirty-two years. She is blessed to be the mother to three awesome sons, and her family has recently welcomed a beautiful daughter-in-law. Ruby is passionate about loving people. She has shared her story to bring hope to the broken hearted. She enjoys helping others and is currently mentoring many women who are walking through their own healing journey.

Seneca Schurbon: Freedom Flowers

I found my business when I was around five years old: imprinting flower frequencies onto water, bottling them, and selling them for 75 cents. It took me another twenty years to take the business seriously. I was looking for some answers for my husband's PTSD and making no progress with traditional methods of talk therapy, medication, and so forth. When you are at your wits' end and haven't slept in days, you'll try anything, even the weird idea that you came up with at five years old.

Flower essences capitalize on flowers' vibrational frequencies to change negative emotional patterns. Each flower heals something different, and they can be ultra-specific. Flower essences can reverse trauma, anxiety, depression, and virtually any pattern of limited or unprofitable thinking.

Even though I have written a book on them, *Flower Power: Essences That Heal*, and have a free mini-course about them on my website, please know that it's not just you with lots of questions. They are still very mysterious to me as well. I'll do my best to give you an overview of how they work. To begin, I base my process on a precedent found in Genesis.

"In the beginning God created the heavens and the earth. Now the earth was formless and empty, darkness was over the surface of the deep, and the Spirit of God was hovering over the waters" Genesis 1:1-2 (NIV).

English doesn't do the creation story justice. It's impossible to translate Hebrew to English without losing essential details. Each word has several meanings as even the characters or "letters" that make up the words possess multiple levels of depth. What I want to point out here is that the word "hover" means to flutter, shake, or vibrate. The Spirit of God was vibrating over the waters, infusing it with divine frequency—fine-tuning the planet that we call home to the vibration and sound of its Creator.

Some Bible scholars believe a lot more happened between the two sentences you read above. This might explain why so little science appears to align with typical creationist beliefs. This might also explain why, on the opening page of the original Hebrew text, the earth appears to have become a total mess (tohuw, meaning chaotic, nothing, confusion, waste, wilderness, empty, formless and vain) after God created it (Strong).

When taking the original Hebrew into closer account, the creation story might read this way: "In the beginning God created the heavens and the earth. Now the earth became chaotic and empty, darkness was over the surface of the deep, and the Spirit of God was vibrating over the waters." We see God covering the earth with water a second time in the Noah story. Other places and writers in the Bible also compare His voice to the sound of water. Psalm 29:3 specifically says the voice of the Lord is over the water. There's something about the water . . . .

Water is a perfect carrier and recorder of frequency. In fact, it's the only substance on earth that can transmit its frequency to everything that comes into contact with it. Recent research confirms water's ability to bridge energetic and physical worlds by accumulating and transferring vibrational patterns and information. It just makes sense that God needed to overwrite the intervening broken pattern that resulted in chaos and darkness in order to restore the planet to His original intent.

Here in essence-making land, I use the same process but add the frequency of flowers. I carefully choose the flowers that I add to water and then I pray over the composition and leave it for the Spirit to hover over. That is, I leave the mixture completely untouched until I literally see light and see that the light is good. In this careful, conscientious, prayerful way, the flower essences that I create are both natural and supernatural.

As a result, my flower essences resonate with the specific healing energy of the flowers I choose and with the energy of Creator. Flower essences vibrate at extremely high frequencies, which works wonders whenever low-frequency vibrational disturbances have taken hold of a person because whenever you introduce a higher frequency to a lower frequency, the lower frequency must yield to the higher frequency. Always. Without exception.

Remember the water? That perfect carrier and recorder of frequency? Our bodies are approximately 70 percent water. Sometimes, old patterns of chaos and darkness need to be overwritten with a new frequency. Our own personal Genesis.

Let's now skip ahead to Eden. I believe that God's original intent was to bring the kingdom of heaven to earth. Throughout the Bible, heaven is referred to as a kingdom. If you managed to stay awake in history class, you know that kingdoms and empires expand their territories in one of two ways: conquest or colonization.

God chose colonization for the earth. Even though a clear and present enemy was on earth, war and conquest weren't part of the game plan. Instead, He did the unexpected: He planted a garden! Inside the garden, He put people and directed them to go forth and multiply. He made a plan for expansion. Eden reflected heaven's atmosphere, government, and culture. There was no sickness, stress, or heartache; there was no decay or corruption. The garden was paradise, heaven on earth. God's plan was as obvious as the garden itself:

occupy earth and expand His kingdom outward "on earth as it is in heaven."

Although the original Eden is no longer a place you can find on a map, it has become even more accessible. Jesus was crystal clear when He said that restoring God's Kingdom on earth no longer has anything to do with a physical dwelling place:

"The kingdom of God cometh not with observation: Neither shall they say, Lo here! or, lo there! for, behold, the kingdom of God is within you." Luke 17:20-21 (KJV).

However, restoring God's indwelling Kingdom simply can't happen as long as people are carrying chaos, destruction, and wounding inside their bodies.

So far, I've made a strong case for water's role in bringing restoration. What about the flowers? Let's take a closer look at the end result of a flower and its purpose for existing.

The flower is the reproductive part of a plant. Its sole purpose is to be fruitful and multiply, and I sense that it's the apex in terms of energy of the plant. Each flower resonates at its trademark specific frequency, which is then transferred to water, the perfect recorder, conductor, and carrier. When you transfer a few drops of a flower essence to a glass of water, your entire glass is encoded with that specific frequency, and every time you take a sip or apply it topically, your body, which is approximately 70 percent water, becomes infused with a specific frequency that can build you up in ways that hundreds of dollars invested in self-help books can't.

As symbolized in the Bible, fruit refers to attitudes and actions as well as to a specific outcome. Paul said the fruit of the Spirit is love, joy, peace, patience, kindness, goodness, faithfulness, gentleness, and self-control (Galatians 5:22-23). Flowers always precede fruit, so it only makes sense that infusing the higher frequency of flowers into water initiates the process that can lead to an idyllic state of being.

Flower essences also make the truth easier to discern. Since truth is essential to attaining peace, most of the time when negative emotions show up, they're the result of believing a lie. A lie in this context is anything that disempowers you, anything that causes you to surrender your potential, and anything that is downright false.

In contrast to the other authors in the book, I rarely deal directly with fragments. You've already heard a bit about the "Fragment Finder" essence, which does what the name says: brings the parts or stored memories to the surface so that you can address them. The action varies from "flushing the bushes" and bringing up a split in your soul that needs to be addressed to spontaneous integration and healing without any effort on your part. Typically, you'll need to employ the techniques in this book or work with someone for help with integration.

Fragment Finder is a great tool although my main mode of working is to address the trauma itself as directly as possible. I've learned that when a person takes an essence, all parts of a person feel it. When I have someone diagnosed with DID who is connecting well with their alters, I can build a combo so that each part receives what they need, hopefully without causing issues for the other parts. Sometimes, I can go straight to the roots of issues with very specific essences; sometimes we have to take a very broad approach and use some stabilization methods first. That last statement is actually true for everyone, regardless of diagnosis.

Most people take flower essences over the long term, although the essences will likely change. By that, I mean that they choose to continue working and fine tuning their healing process by addressing new or more minor issues. A flower essence should not be like taking the same vitamin indefinitely. My intention is for you to always be progressing and not needing the last essence you took. While some deeply rooted issues take longer to heal, you should eventually be able to quit using essences without reverting back to an unhealed state.

My best advice for those reading this book is to use essences in conjunction with inner healing and deliverance. I truly believe that the strongest advantage comes when you use all three in conjunction.

For more information on flower essences and how they can help you, please visit my website at www.freedom-flowers.com.

Diane Moyer: DeBalm Ministries

For years, I received the same prophetic word: "You've been hurt and are very wounded." Whoever was prophesying then prayed for me and sent me on my merry way. However, my life never changed. I went to the next special meeting and heard the same word and received the same prayer. Nothing changed. This continued for over ten years! Finally one day, after receiving the same word yet again and as tears of frustration flowed down my face, this prophet didn't pray for me. Instead, he continued. He told me to seek Christian counseling and then God would open up the whole world to me. Finally, I had firm directions that I acted upon as soon as I could.

As I went to counseling at a church ninety minutes away, I also attended their training. They were teaching "Restoring the Foundations" by Chester and Betsy Kylstra. I completely absorbed their material, resulting in an amazing transformation. The Lord healed me of so many ungodly beliefs, giving my belief system a major overhaul. Many, including my pastor at the time, noticed the difference. My pastor soon requested that I teach the course at my church.

Although I had many areas that were healed, other areas still needed continued healing. I had a lot of rejection in my life. I noticed that the Lord healed some of these wounds as I entered into intimate worship with Him. This started to give me further insight into how our hurts and wounds are healed.

In a few years, the Lord led me to join Isaiah 61 Ministries. I initially sat under Dr. Steve Mory, a Christian psychiatrist who taught me a lot about prayer ministry. He also gave me the opportunity to go through the Advanced Theophostic Training where I learned more about DID/SRA. My first year at Isaiah, I ministered to eight women with this diagnosis.

When Dr. Mory moved out of town, the director of Isaiah, John Kowalczyk, became my mentor. He flowed with ease in the Holy Spirit, and I learned that I didn't need to have the answers. God had them, and He was always faithful to reveal them in each session. The pressure was off me and on the Lord. I have continued that perspective in ministry.

In 2009, the Lord led me to start DeBalm Ministries. I had a prophetic word at the beginning of the year that God would set me in my own ministry by July 31. Sure enough, He did just that and quite miraculously! I didn't do anything to initiate it.

Since it began, DeBalm has focused on setting people free via personal ministry, training programs, and group sessions.

Author's Collective Note: We are sorry to say that Diane passed away on June 6, 2018 after an accident and lengthy medical battle. Her teaching materials remain available on her website, in this book, and in the books she coauthored with Matt Evans. She was a blessing to all who knew her.

Matt Evans

I regularly pray with people for many kinds of healing and especially have a heart to equip others to be effective at miraculously resolving deeper issues. The stories that I have included in this book have probably given you some insight into what my ministry can look like.

I differ a bit from your typical minister. I'm not interested in a fancy title or a big ceremonial hat. I prefer organic relationships over large organizations and prestigious networks. I relate to people in a low-key manner and on equal footing. I take an aggressive stance when it comes to standing for the miraculous and taking ground from the enemy, but I aspire to go low, to serve others in an environment of freedom.

God has shown me that He is love. I believe that true spiritual authority is simply loving people, serving under them to build them up, and activating them in their own authority rather than bossing them around with mine, as Jesus advised in Matthew 20:25-26.

I've always been a bit outside the box, and have struggled at times with not fitting into church and ministry crowds. During those seasons, I wondered how my intense passion to see the kingdoms of this world become the Kingdom of our God could possibly find a channel for release, that is, without requiring me to be someone I'm not.

Amidst feeling like the misfit and the unlikely one far too often, I've found the Lord faithful to miraculously open doors for me and to accomplish many significant things beyond my wildest expectations.

I've come to love being a part of this journey, being a part of building a kingdom not of this world, a kingdom being established by the One who is by far the most beautiful thing I've ever experienced.

I have a website at http://for-healingthenations.com that lists my various books and blog posts as well as contact information. *Divine Healing for Spirit, Soul, and Body*, which I co-authored with Diane Moyer, is our first written work, and I highly recommend it if you are interested in learning more about what we do and how the Lord has revealed His heart to us.

All of the books I've been able to find on the subject of ministering to parts have focused only on the most intense end of the dissociation spectrum, those who have been ritually abused and who suffer from DID. One of the main reasons we've written this book was to fill the void of material about how to minister to common fractured parts as opposed to only the most extreme cases and to fill the void of material on how to apply the power of the Holy Spirit to heal wounded parts as opposed to relying mostly on human psychological techniques.

Still, I consider a number of books already written to be very helpful, even brilliant. Truly, as we progress into more difficult cases, we are going to need all the help we can get.

Written in everyday language, *Help for the Fractured Soul: Experiencing Healing and Deliverance from Deep Trauma* by Candyce Roberts offers a great and balanced overview of wisdom when working with severe cases.

Restoring the Shattered Self: A Christian Counselor's Guide to Complex Trauma, by Heather Davediuk Gingrich also provides great insight into these issues. It is written in psychological terms with the professional therapist in mind and contains a wealth of wisdom from one counselor's lifetime of working with severe trauma.

The early discussion on relational safety and ethics is invaluable and references much further reading on the subject. The author shares strong insight into connecting and communicating with fractured parts.

Healing the Unimaginable: Treating Ritual Abuse and Mind Control by Allison Miller is an extensive examination of many of the complexities of working with survivors of RA. Not for the faint of heart, this book includes tremendous insight into what RA survivors have been through and what recovery might look like.

Dan Duval of Bride Ministries also has a lot of audio material freely available online about how he ministers to RA and DID. He has also gathered a small network of healers working in that area.

Arthur Burk has audio materials and blog posts relevant to working with parts as well. His three part mp3 series Tools for Freedom, found on his Austrian website, goes especially deep into the subject.

Michael C. King: The Kings of Eden

My wife and I started The Kings of Eden, LLC in 2014 after I had tried unsuccessfully to start a number of network marketing businesses. I both love the idea of people helping people and creating wealth, but the methods in those businesses were too much of a cult-like lifestyle for me. Instead, we decided to launch a platform for my books, and I share a weekly blog as well. I have always been a writer, even writing fantasy stories in middle and high school in my free time, and as the years have gone by, my love for writing has not changed. However, I have shifted most of my writing to spiritual themes.

At www.thekingsofeden.com, you will find a myriad of encouraging and uplifting articles, covering many topics including but not limited to faith, miracles, prophecy and spiritual gifts, angels, raising the dead and immortality, deliverance and inner healing, spirit travel, physical healing and divine-healing prayer, and much more. My goal in this area is to help encourage the Body of Christ through cutting-edge teaching that pushes the boundaries yet which has practical application for life. I have published six books to date not counting this collaboration and have a library-full of books in my head waiting to make it to print on all of the topics listed above. All of my books can be found on Amazon.com under the name Michael C. King, and our website, thekingsofeden.com, has links to social media so that you can connect further.

Another major focus of my heart is the desire for us to live in the abundant life that Jesus promised us in John 10:10. In addition to spiritual teaching on healing, resurrection, and eternal life, we understand the practical need for concrete help with physical and emotional healing, which is why our website is constantly expanding into new areas of health and wellness. We have begun to partner with Freedom Flowers to produce gemstone essences from gems that have all appeared supernaturally from heaven. All of these gem essences are designed to help resolve negative and even harmful emotions that hinder personal wellness.

Works Cited

"Bone Marrow." Encyclopædia Britannica. Ed. Encyclopædia
      Britannica Editors. Encyclopædia Britannica, 29 Jan. 2016.
      Web. 1 July 2017.

"Chronic Pain." American Chronic Pain Association. American
      Chronic Pain Association, n.d. Web. 7 June 2017.
      <https://theacpa.org/glossary>.

Dizdar, Russ. "Interview with Russ Dizdar." Personal interview. Apr.
      2004.

Dube, Shanta R. et al. "Cumulative Childhood Stress and Autoim-
      mune Diseases in Adults." Psychosomatic Medicine 71.2
      (2009): 243–250. PMC. Web. 2 July 2017.

Hanson, J. W. The Greek word Aiōn-aiōnios: translated everlasting,
      eternal in the Holy Bible, shown to denote limited duration.
      Chicago: Hanson, 1878. Print.

Murray, Richard K. The Question of Hell. Dalton, GA: Createspace,
      2007. Print.

Strong, James. Strong's Exhaustive Concordance. Peabody, MA:
      Hendrickson, 2007. Blueletterbible.com. Web. 2016-17.

Tortora, Gerard Joseph, and Bryan Derrickson. Principles of
      Anatomy and Physiology. New York: Wiley, 2006. Print.

Made in the USA
Middletown, DE
22 September 2021